CONCILIUM
Religion in the Seventies

CONCILIUM

POLARIZATION IN THE CHURCH

Edited by

Hans Kung and
Walter Kasper

Herder and Herder

1973
HERDER AND HERDER NEW YORK
815 Second Avenue
New York 10017

ISBN: 0–8164–2572–8

Cum approbatione Ecclesiastica

Library of Congress Catalog Card Number: 73–6435

Printed in the United States

CONTENTS

Editorial

The Danger of Parties in the Church

Concilium is not a party and has no wish to be a party. Looking through what will soon be ten years' issues of our journal, one is amazed by the variety of opinions from many different countries, churches, orders, disciplines and tendencies. Our journal is quite independent. It is the work of theologians who are committed to the mission of Jesus Christ and to the renewal of the Church initiated by Vatican II and who welcome any constructive theological contribution.

In its very name, *Concilium* is committed as much to the unity as to the diversity of the Church. By presenting honest and expert discussion of problems and positive theological solutions, and by avoiding pseudo-orthodox tedium and wild extremism, our journal hopes both to stimulate and to integrate. This is a hard road for us theologians, but it is perhaps not too much to claim that, while *Concilium* has certainly never chosen the safer course, neither has it given way to the temptation to live too dangerously.

None the less, we cannot be blind to the sad fact that in the Church in recent years, as in society in general, tensions have increased, polarizations have sharpened and conflicts have become more bitter. We do not believe that there will be a new division in the Church. Today's exodus takes the form not of a revolution against authority but of a silent departure.

But we do speak more today than in the past of different camps within the same Church, of conservatives and progressives, pre-conciliar and post-conciliar Catholics, and so on. The question of pluralism is being raised in a new form. What, for example, is the place of pluralism in the Church, and what are its limits? Should there really be different movements in the Church and in its dioceses and parishes? Some Christians see everything through conservative, others through revolutionary, eyes. Can organized parties or groups really exist in the Church? Some Christians give an emphatically negative reply to this question, while others simply ask "Why not?"

It is a complex question, and we have invited sociologists, political scientists, exegetes, historians and dogmatic and pastoral theologians to contribute towards a solution. This has resulted in many different diagnoses, points of view and distinctions—perhaps so much material that the question is in danger of getting lost. It is quite true that each issue of *Concilium* is a small book.

In an effort to help the reader find his way, and to indicate where the various views converge, we have tried something new in this issue. One of the two editorial directors has gone through the various contributions and produced a summary under various headings, in an attempt to clarify and stimulate discussion.

WALTER KASPER
HANS KÜNG

PART I
ARTICLES

Theodor Eschenburg

The Function of a Political Party

THIS essay offers no more than a partial description. It limits itself to a few characteristic phenomena of Western democracies, with their two-party or multi-party systems.

1. Specific features

There are many definitions of parties, but they often omit to distinguish parties from other organizations which are like them in subsidiary features. In legal language, parties may perhaps be defined in the following passage from the party law of the German Federal Republic: "Associations of citizens who, either permanently or for a substantial period, in the territory of the Federal Republic or of a *Land* [federal region], wish to influence the taking of political decisions and wish to take part in representing the people in the German Bundestag [federal parliament] or in a Landtag [regional parliament]. They must offer a guarantee of the seriousness of their aims in all aspects of their actual situation, particularly in the scale and solidity of their organization, the number of their members and the character of their public appearances. Only natural persons can be members of parties." This legal definition enables administrative and legal authorities to distinguish between parties with their privileges (protection from dissolution and financial support from the state) and other organizations not entitled to recognition as parties.

A sociological definition of the party in a parliamentary democracy might include the following factors:

1. The principal aim of a party is to assume government or continue in government.

2. A secondary aim of a party is to achieve particular goals and to prevent the achievement of other parties' goals with which it disagrees.

3. It puts forward persons (candidates) and programmes at elections.

4. For these purposes it must have a permanent organization.

All parties have a conception of the common good, though these conceptions differ according to the different interests which dominate them. Associations, on the other hand, represent the interests of particular sectors, and to promote these interests they seek to influence parties. Parties are expected to be able to take up a position on any political question, whereas associations are only interested in politics in so far as interests of their members are concerned which it is their job as associations to defend. A trade union, however, as well as defending the wide-ranging particular class and professional interests of its members, may take up a position on general political questions, such as foreign and defence policy. A taxpayers' association is interested in all political matters which lead to expenditure, but only in the furtherance of its aim of keeping the tax burden as low as possible. Churches also belong to the category of associations to the extent that their interests intrude into the secular sphere (e.g., church tax, denominational schools, the banning of sporting events during divine service). A professional group may divide into associations with different party affiliations, as with the Christian and Socialist trade unions in Germany before 1933, the Christian, Socialist, Communist and neo-Fascist trade unions of Italy, and the Dutch Catholic, Calvinist and lay industrial associations. Conversely, interest groups may form in parties and have strong sympathy with the corresponding associations. There can also be "interest parties", parliamentary extensions of particular associations, but so far these have been short-lived.

The constant readiness to put forward parliamentary candidates and secure their election is an important criterion of a party. For this purpose it is not important that an association may secure the adoption of one of its members or officials as a party's parliamentary candidate. He can only be a candidate when the party adopts him. Usually (though not in the United Kingdom) only parties may put forward parliamentary candidates.

2. *The Origin of parties*

Parties came into being during the wave of constitutionalism in the nineteenth century with the establishment of elected popular representation, and became an essential institution in the constitutional state. In the states of continental Europe which lived under enlightened absolutism and had more or less vigorous feudal structures, the initiative for the abolition of the old state form and the construction of a constitutional system involving the sharing of power came from the liberals after the French Revolution. The liberals' activity in organizing movements and forming parties forced the reluctant conservatives, who defended the *status quo*, to form parties themselves.

The opposition between the desire to preserve and the desire to change constitutional and socio-political systems is still an essential criterion by which parties may be distinguished, and reappears continually in constantly changing political situations. Parties are described as being on the right or on the left. This description goes back to the seating arrangements in the French Estates of 1789, the predecessor of the French National Assembly; the nobles were seated on the right and the commoners on the left of the president. There frequently formed, between the conservative and "progressive" groups, a centre, itself divided into numerous tendencies, which was at one time closer to the right and at another closer to the left.

In a two-party system the left wing of the right-wing party and the right wing of the left-wing party frequently draw together. In a multi-party system one or more distinct centre parties may be formed; this arrangement is not static. The original opposition was between liberals and conservatives. Then, after 1848, when the Socialist movements and parties emerged as the representatives of the underprivileged, and in the first place of wage-earners, and called for constitutional changes in opposition to the conservatives and liberals, the liberals were pushed towards the centre. This arrangement into right, centre and left can be seen more or less clearly in both most parliaments and in individual parties and groups. In certain circumstances divisions within parties can lead to splits.

3. *Beginnings in Britain and America*

The British parliament of the eighteenth and the first quarter of the nineteenth century was, as a result of very strict financial qualifications for the franchise, representative only of the upper class. Only the propertied classes had the vote. As the franchise was increasingly extended to increasingly broader sectors of the population, the two parliamentary groups, the Tories and the Whigs—the predecessors of the Conservatives and the Liberals, who began as tightly-knit cliques—developed an interest in winning support for the candidates among voters through formal organizations, i.e., parties. The third British Party, the Labour Party, was a democratic foundation. In contrast to the Socialist parties of continental Europe, it is unaffected by Marxist theories and developed out of the Fabian Society, an anti-radical and anti-liberal association of intellectuals, and the trade unions. Before 1914 Labour won parliamentary seats only with the help of the Liberals, but after World War I it supplanted them.

In the American Constitutional Convention of Philadelphia in 1787, a conference of delegates from individual states, the first differences were regional, between the agricultural south and the industrial north. With its reliance on Rousseau's doctrines, the Convention believed that parties in parliament and as organizations of voters were superfluous, and indeed harmful. In their view the most respected residents of an electoral district or the most respected members of the state parliaments should become deputies. A small circle of the upper class nominated the candidates. In opposition to the aristocratic landowning group under Washington, the Federalists, another group, the Republicans, grew up under Jefferson. In opposition to the aristocratic selection of candidates, rather than encouraging those excluded from the governmental process to make themselves felt by another method of nominating candidates, the Republicans tried to establish a more democratic ideology, which soon revealed tensions between different interests. This was the beginning of the party system in the United States. In the course of time the Federalists were also forced to create a party apparatus. The formation of the modern parties, the Republicans and Democrats, did not begin until the end of the 1820s; it was stimulated by the urge to absorb the increasing numbers of immigrants as new voters. These parties were "rival patronage concerns", with no clear programmes. Their most effective means of propaganda was their ability to provide their voters with jobs in the public service if they won (the spoil system). There is still no tightly organized party structure, and electoral propaganda is left in the hands of successful business bosses.

4. Beginnings in Germany

In the German elections to the Frankfurt National Assembly of 1848, there were no organized parties in the usual sense, and people rather than programmes were the main feature. The arguments which emerged during the discussions in the National Assembly led to the formation of groups as a means of avoiding fragmentation in discussions and votes. Members of the various groups met in particular inns and at first named the groups after them. In the course of time the groups developed into parties, first, after the failure of the attempt to form an Empire in 1848, in the individual states, often through the formation of local election committees.

5. British and American and Continental European parties

In Britain and the United States the two-party system has lasted, with temporary deviations, until the present. The main determining factor was that decisions were from the beginning made by popular election, in the United States for the selection of a president and in Britain to form a government. On the other hand, the Continental parties were limited to legislation, which needed the monarch's approval. The monarch also appointed a government in his own right, independently of parliament. The failure of the rival claims to rule, and the purely legislative activity of the parties, permitted the formation of changing and often temporary legislative coalitions and thus prepared the way for the appearance of a multi-party system. The parties were not, as in Britain and the United States, principal actors, set on governing, but supporting figures, associations based on common effort and outlook under the influence of a specific philosophy.

The first party programmes could be called party philosophies; they started from a particular view of man against a background of a particular range of social interests.

In the German Empire, social stratification and differing religious beliefs led to the formation of four main ideological groups. Three of these were non-Catholic, and tended to divide into parties separated by various subtle distinctions: the Liberals and the Conservatives, who were subdivided into parties of a more conservative and a more democratic tendency, and the Socialists.

6. *Denominational parties*

In addition to the foregoing, there was the big Catholic defensive Centre Party; it had no programme and was therefore flexible, but tended to follow Catholic social teaching. Between 1870 and 1913 it occupied a middle position between right and left and was the one "linking party", without which no majority could be formed. At the same time it was the only popular party, since it included Catholics of all social classes, welded firmly together by the pressure of strict religious discipline. It was expected that the practising Catholic would belong only to Catholic associations, and this led to a separate Catholic society, which even Catholics called "the ghetto". Until 1919 there was no real party organization, though rudimentary regional organizations and local committees existed, the latter mainly led by priests. Priests also acted as unpaid party secretaries, and when necessary met the costs of the modest local expenditure out of church funds. The Centre was a parliamentary group without a party. Its highest authority in the country as a whole was the executive of the Reichstag party, and in the individual states the executives of the Centre groups in the state parliaments.

Catholic parties with various secular aims and other differences have existed since 1889 in the pluralist Netherlands and since 1830 in the Catholic provinces of Belgium. There has been a Catholic party in Italy on the German model since 1918, and there was one with class tendencies in Imperial Austria until 1918, which continued after World War I as a conservative party in the Republic. These Catholic parties, which unreservedly accepted the internal structure of their Church with the pope at its head, were called "Ultramontane".

Two competing Reformed parties exist in the Netherlands. Three attempts have been made in Germany to set up Evangelical parties, each time unsuccessfully. The doctrines and structure of the Evangelical Church, unlike those of the Catholic Church, have not encouraged party formation.

With the introduction of parliamentary systems in which parties formed governments and took over responsibility for government, political programmes pushed philosophical principles into the background, though there were occasional tendencies in the opposite direction (the rebirth of ideology). Generally the establishment of a parliamentary system made no fundamental change in the traditional party system. Coalitions have frequently been necessary, with more or less pronounced signs of crisis, as in the third and fourth French Republics, in the Weimar Republic and at present in Italy, the Netherlands and Belgium.

7. Totalitarian parties

After World War I, radical parties came into being on the extreme right and extreme left. Germany and Italy had totalitarian monolithic parties, the National Socialists and Fascists under "charismatic leaders" (Hitler and Mussolini) on the one hand, and the Communists on the other. These parties were bitter opponents of parliamentary democracy, and were therefore not potential coalition partners. Taking advantage of the growing hostility to the parties among the people, they crushed the existing party system between them and destroyed the constitutional structure. The Fascist dictatorships banned all other parties, as the Russian Communists had done, but in Germany, Austria and Italy this produced no more than an interruption in the continuity of the parties.

8. After 1945

Hitler's campaign against the two main Churches led to a reduction of the old bitter denominational hostility in Germany and made a major contribution to the founding after the collapse of a trans-denominational party, the Christian Democratic Union

(CDU), which absorbed many of the elements of the old Centre. The plan to form a party combining Protestant and Catholic Christians goes back to the nineteenth century. The organizational model for the formation of the CDU was provided by the Christian trade unions, which included both Catholic and Protestant workers and had existed since the turn of the century. The present West German three-party system (CDU, FDP, SDP) still shows traditional elements from the period 1870–1913.

After the collapse the Austrian People's Party and the Italian Christian Democrats emerged in 1945–1946 in their previous form, but with a broader social base and more powerful internal tensions. The Italian party especially is an example of the extent to which parties on the wings can determine the internal structure and degree of consensus in a centre party.

9. Parties of notables, integrating parties and popular parties

As well as being a preliminary to parliamentary activity, party formation can also be a result of it. Elected political decision-making bodies which meet regularly, even if not continuously, during their term of office inevitably produce groups and parties where these did not exist before the election. The introduction of parliament and party formation influence each other. Generally, it is impossible for there to be parties without a parliament or parliaments without parties. Parties may develop out of cliques, clubs and movements. Election committees produced parties of notables: a relatively small number of local or regional notables who organized election campaigns on a voluntary basis. These have also been called voters' parties. The first mass parties, which have also been called integrating parties, were the Socialist parties, which were first overwhelmingly workers' parties. These tried to make all their supporters party members and to weld them together by democratically strict party discipline. A member of the German Social Democratic Party was not, in theory, allowed to be a member of any organization other than Socialist ones, a rule which extended to such things as choirs, sports clubs, educational associations and women's associations. In the German Empire this developed into a "Socialist alternative society". The integrating parties were the first to develop their own party bureaucracies. The parties of notables also came more and more to rely on bureaucracies, and the larger ones tried to develop into integrating parties. Today in West Germany, however, party members are still no more than about 3 per cent of voters. The dominant tendency in the two main West German parties (CDU and SPD) since the war has been to develop into popular parties: parties which draw their membership, though perhaps in different proportions, from all classes of the population. Popular parties must try to reconcile conflicting interests, while allowing some greater influence than others. This can give rise to conflicts between the parties and interest groups associated with them; examples from West Germany are those between the SPD and the West German trade union organization (DGB), whose membership is overwhelmingly Social Democratic, and between the CDU and the farmers' association traditionally associated with it.

It has become clear that the voting system alone does not determine the form of the party system, although a simple majority system favours the maintenance of a two-party system and proportional voting encourages the development of a multi-party system. Under the system of personified proportional representation which operates in West Germany, only parties which either win 5 per cent of the total vote or win seats in three constituencies are entitled to an allocation of seats in proportion to their votes. A number of small parties have been eliminated by this blocking clause, and only one, the Free Democratic Party (FDP), has succeeded in recovering. This restriction also, in combination with the system of state financing, which is always based on the results of the last election, makes the formation of new parties more difficult, and this can sharpen the tensions within the existing ones.

10. Parties and parliamentary parties

Over a long period, parliamentary groups cannot exist without extra-parliamentary parties. Just as parliamentary groups are the essential prerequisite for the effectiveness of parliaments, so parties are the indispensable electoral organizations of the parliamentary parties. If the parliamentary party is the executive organ of the whole party, the larger party is at least the propaganda organ of the parliamentary party. Each depends on the other;

the actions of the representatives in parliament are the criterion by which the voters sought by the party have to judge. On the other hand, the party's general principles and its successive election manifestos lay down a guide-line for the policy of the members in parliament. The party is a check on the parliamentary group.

The different functions of national party and parliamentary group, responsibility for the programme on the one hand, and responsibility for parliamentary decisions on the other, lead to a conflict of interests with regard to the overall leadership. Legally the party may not give the parliamentary group instructions, but it can exercise a stronger or weaker influence on the composition of the group through the selection of election candidates. Sometimes the decisions of party conferences, or more often party executives or presidia, have a general binding force for the policy of the parliamentary group. In following them, however, the parliamentary party has considerable latitude, and this is increased when the party is part of a coalition with another or several parliamentary parties. The same effect is produced by the parliamentary party's need to take account of day-to-day considerations of parliamentary tactics. There have been cases in which parliamentary parties have yielded to decisions of the larger party with which they disagreed, and cases in which they have acted in striking contravention of clear party decisions. Between the two extremes, in which the party is merely the tool of the parliamentary group, or vice versa, there is a wide range of positions. The tension is highest when a majority of party activists in the country are in opposition to a majority of the parliamentary group.

In the classical schema of English parliamentarism, the parliamentary party, whether in government or opposition, leads the party in the country, and the parliamentary party is led by the prime minister or the leader of the opposition, as the case may be, who is elected by the parliamentary party (as "leader of the party"). There is therefore a personal union between the leadership of the government or opposition and party leadership. The party can, however, call for the leader's resignation (as the Conservatives called for Chamberlain's in 1940 and Eden's in 1957). More recently there have been signs in the Labour Party under

Harold Wilson's leadership of a tendency to strengthen the influence of the party in the country in relation to the parliamentary party. In this connection it must be remembered that the British Labour Party has not only individual members—the only sort allowed by law to West German parties—but also corporate members, notably the trade unions, which have a very strong position at party conferences. Adenaeur tried to lead the CDU on the English model, and largely succeeded until 1959. In foreign policy he made the decisions himself, and in domestic policy he took account of tendencies within the party, trying to maintain a balance between interests, and of electoral considerations, while identifying himself with specific desires and aims. Adenauer was Chancellor and party leader. More recently efforts have been made to separate the party chairmanship and the candidacy for the chancellorship. In Italy de Gasperi was simultaneously head of the government and leader of the Christian Democratic Party from 1945 to 1954. The process of forming a coalition with either left or right, which was made necessary by Christian Democrat electoral losses, led to a permanent leadership crisis, and this was expressed in the separation of the two posts.

11. *Party organization*

Parties need a convenient way of informing a broad range of the electorate about events in the party and its parliamentary group. This can be done through party daily papers, or through daily papers which differ in political outlook and in degrees of commitment and are not tied to any particular party. Other channels are party periodicals and journals, though these are mostly read only by members and very interested supporters. The main channel is radio and television. Television provides perhaps the most effective news service. During election campaigns all these channels are overshadowed by propaganda campaigns, which use techniques derived from commercial advertising.

The activity of modern parties is very expensive, if only on account of their permanent bureaucracies. Expenses are covered by contributions from members, donations, and, in many countries, by financial support from the state, in proportion to the position of the parties at the last election.

12. Competition between parties

In democracies, decisions are made as the result of the conflict of parties, which is often preceded by a conflict in the individual parties. Parties both represent the people and activate the voters. They give expression to the popular will not so much by investigating it as by offering the voters rival long-term and short-term aims and candidates. Freedom of competition among parties is a necessary condition for the operation of the system of representative democracy. The competitive struggle also produces many phenomena which are undesirable or even shocking. To mention only one, free elections are not possible without political propaganda, which is often vulgar. Competition between the parties, and between groups and individuals within the parties, operates at the level of direct election, in parliament and in the government, and also on the three levels of party organization, the local group, the regional party and the national party. It is one of the main influences on a political system in which decisions are made chiefly by political parties.

Competition between the parties may develop an impetus of its own which the wider organization, in this case the state, has very little power to check. Only where the bulk of the parties and their supporters, in spite of their differences, accept the political system and the procedures and authority of its institutions can a supra-party peace set limits to the party battle. Where the bulk of the parties or a large minority lacks this loyalty to the system, the system itself is threatened, as can be seen from the Weimar Republic.

The rivalry between parties in the struggle for voters and for a majority in parliament means that the parties also influence each other's attitudes. This means the whole range of debate between the parties in a particular state can move at one time to the right and at another to the left.

While it is the function of parties to express the popular will, they have also to remember that the only possible positions with regard to a measure in parliament, apart from abstention, are a vote for or against. This means that when a party seeks to win a majority of members for one of its proposals, it can only propose a single solution. This in turn means that it has to limit opinion formation in its ranks.

13. *Parties as a model for extra-parliamentary democracy*

Ever since the movement for the extension of democracy made its mark and spread, the question has been asked whether the model of the political party, perhaps in other combinations of tendencies and other forms, is really suitable for the further institutionalization of democracy in the wide and complex area which lies outside parliament.

Associations, especially the larger ones, have internal groupings, sometimes with party sympathies, though most of them do not last long. Student parties have formed since students began to elect representatives to the governing bodies of universities and colleges and to student parliaments. These are sometimes connected with existing parties, though usually to their left, and sometimes, especially on the left, are separate, often very small, groups. In general they have not acquired permanent form, and the constant change in membership of the student body makes this difficult. Interest in elections is sometimes very low.

14. *Parties in the Church?*

Movements, and struggles between them, have certainly existed in the Catholic Church, and have emerged even outside councils. It is, however, perhaps wrong to speak of parties or party-like formations in a Church with a traditionally heavily authoritarian and hierarchical structure and no parliamentary or similar institutions. Nevertheless it is not unreasonable to assume that the setting up of collegial and synodal bodies in the post-conciliar period will inevitably lead, sooner or later, to the appearance of parties even in the Catholic Church.

The situation in the Protestant Church is different, as can be seen from the case of Germany. Even under the system of control by local rulers, the Evangelical Church in Germany began during the nineteenth century to change its organization to one modelled on secular constitutionalism. Associations representing interests in the Church came into existence with the synods. "There was a right and a left, and sometimes also a centre, in the Church, based on fundamental attitudes to the main points of the Church's faith.... In view of the relationship between ecclesiastical and political conservatism and liberalism, it is not surprising that differences of opinion in politics should also have had an effect" (J. Beckmann, "Kirchliche Parteien in Deutschland", *Religion in Geschichte und Gegenwart* 5 [1961], Col. 129).

With the end of the old system of princely control in 1918, the Evangelical Church chose a form of organization based on the parliamentary democracy of the new German constitution. The synods or congresses of the churches in the individual states had the role of parliaments. There were elections, though mainly indirect, on the proportional or list system. This assumed the existence of parties, which, unlike political parties, had fluid boundaries and no clear policies. At the beginning of the 1930s the movement known as the "German Christians" was formed. It called for the formation of a "Reich Church on a Lutheran pattern" which would have as members only Christians "of Aryan race" and would recognize the sovereignty of the National Socialist state "by faith". The movement won a majority at the church elections in July 1933, and with the regime's support took over control of the Church. The opposition movement in the Church, the "Confessing Church", rejected the idea of a church party absolutely on theological grounds: "As the community of Christ, the Church cannot organize itself into parties to form community leaderships and synods, since party divisions contradict the nature of the community.... Party divisions in the Church are not a structural principle which is necessary or applicable to the formation and work of synods of the Church" (Beckmann, *loc. cit.*). The author of this quotation was himself a member of the Confessing Church.

Many would agree that political parties, with their rough tactics and loud propaganda, are not an appropriate model for church communities. The view has repeatedly been expressed at synods that party formation contravenes the provisions of the Augsburg Confession of 1555, by which the Lutheran Church is obliged *consentire de doctrina*.

In order to prevent the formation of parties, the indirect and proportional voting system was replaced after 1945 by direct election on a simple majority: "Participation in the election is not just the exercise of the rights of a church member, but the exercise of the priesthood of all believers in the responsibility of faith as an act of service in and for the community" (Wendt, "Kirchen-wahlen", *Religion in Geschichte und Gegenwart* 3 [1969], col. 1596). Direct election is limited to the election of elders and the local parish council. State synods are elected from members of regional and local synods, and sometimes from parish councils; a process of selection operates. It is hard to prevent attempts to form parties in the synods, and their existence has an effect on the elections, which can encourage their formation and consolidation.

On the other hand, the setting up of representative bodies to be filled by direct election depends on the possibility of forming parties. Without parties, mass elections are impossible. The formation of a representative body to be elected directly by all those working in radio and television has often been considered, but so far the idea has collapsed for lack of any suitable model for party formation.

There have been frequent demands for the direct election of the EEC parliament by the populations of the Common Market countries. There would be no difficulty for the different parties of the individual countries in presenting candidates for election. Party groups already exist in the EEC parliament, which are joined by parties with related attitudes from different countries, but they have little importance because of the EEC parliament's lack of authority to take decisions. As soon as it acquired real authority—and only then would direct election be worth while—support for the policies of individual EEC parliamentary groups within national parties could do great damage at subsequent national elections. Severe crises, perhaps resulting in splits, within particular national parties could not be ruled out. There is also the converse danger, that the EEC parliamentary groups would be split by their various members' fears of the effect of group policies on elections.

The question of parties in the Church is bound up with the Church's view of itself, but is also clearly determined by particular sociological "laws".

Translated by Francis McDonagh

Rudolf Pesch

Were there Parties in the New Testament Church?

THE equivalent in New Testament Greek for our term "party", in the sense of a school, a movement within a school, a doctrine or a breakaway group, is *hairesis*, the term which was later used pejoratively to describe a (heretical) sect (*secta*) or heresy.[1] In Jewish terms, the Christians could be regarded as one of the different Jewish parties, such as that of the Sadducees (cf. Acts 5. 17; Josephus, *Ant.* 13, 171; 20, 199, etc.) or the Pharisees (cf. Acts 15. 5; Josephus, *Bell. Iud.* II, 8. 14), as "the sect of the Nazarenes" (Acts 24. 5; cf. Justin, *Dial.* 17, 1; 108, 2), though one which was increasingly "spoken against" in Judaism (Acts 28. 22), and given a negative evaluation as a sect. In Acts 24. 14, for example, the way (*hodos*) according to which Paul worships the God of their fathers is called *hairesis*. Within Judaism parties were groups which adopted a position of their own on particular questions without denying each other's legitimate position within Judaism (as that of the Samaritans, who were treated as a sect, was denied). Other *haireseis* are, for Clement of Alexandria, the philosophical schools, based on a system of *dogmata* (rational knowledge, *Strom.* VII, 5. 16), and, for Justin (*Apol.* 1, 7. 3), the Marcionites, though in this case a Christian sect.[2]

Is it possible to distinguish *haireseis* in the New Testament

---

[1] Cf. P. Geoltrain, "Partei, Sekte", *Bibl. Hist. Handwörterbuch* III, pp. 1391–4; H. Schlier, *TWNT* I, pp. 179–84; M. Simon, *Die jüdischen Sekten zur Zeit Christi* (Einsiedeln, Zürich, Cologne, 1964).

[2] Cf. M. Elze, "Der Begriff des Dogmas in der Alter Kirche", *Zeitschrift für Theologie und Kirche* 61 (1964), pp. 421–38, esp. pp. 425 f.

Church, groups with clearly differentiated "positions"? Were there even in the New Testament period parties which as sects were refused communion with the Church because they themselves refused to accept it? This short article will try to assemble the most important New Testament data before finally attempting to formulate an answer to the question of the legitimacy of parties in the Church.

I. Hebrews and Hellenists

As we learn from Acts 6 (and further information which can be combined with that), the "primitive" Jerusalem community existed at an early period in two groups which differed not only in their language but even more in their "theology" and "constitution". These were the "Hebrews" and the "Hellenists" (Acts 6. 1).

The "Hebrews" were the group of Aramaic-speaking Christians who gathered round the "Galileans" who went up to Jerusalem again after Easter (Acts 1. 11; 2. 7); the leaders of this group were Simon Peter and the Twelve. Even as followers of the Messiah Jesus, whose imminent return they expected, they remained "within the limits of obedience to the Jewish law and the temple worship".[3] They revived Jesus' claim to be the representative of the eschatological Israel and carried out missionary activity among their fellow Jews. They took the law as the basis of their discussion with their Jewish brethren. James, the brother of the Lord, emerged as their particular advocate, and soon came to be the leader of the primitive Hebrew community.

The "Hellenists" were Jews (mostly from the Diaspora) whose mother-tongue was Greek and who had been won for Jesus. They grouped themselves—perhaps with the synagogue as their model—around the Seven led by Stephen. In the preaching of Jesus as it had been handed down and in faith in him they discovered features which "meant much to them" as Jews from the Diaspora "and which they missed elsewhere in Jerusalem. These were ideas such as that it is not food which makes a man unclean

---

[3] H. Köster, "*ΓΝΩΜΑΙ ΔΙΑΦΟΡΟΙ*. Ursprung und Wesen der Mannigfaltigkeit in der Geschichte des frühen Christentums", *Zeitschrift für Theologie und Kirche* 65 (1968), p. 166.

but what comes out of his heart, or that the commandment to love one's neighbour daily is greater than the other commandments, even keeping the sabbath. Jesus' criticisms of the temple worship and a view of Jesus' death as an expiation for the forgiveness of sins made the temple and its liturgy superfluous, and the interpretation of the resurrection as the dawn of the last days made it possible to replace the Torah of Moses with a new and purely ethical, 'Messianic' Torah, which could draw on Jesus' explicit criticism of the law. And not least, the experience of the prophetic spirit freed them from their ties to the letter of the law and the casuistic attitudes of scribal learning."[4] With their critiques of the temple and the law, the "Hellenists" put forward what was for the "Hebrews" a completely revolutionary view of faith in Christ. Even Luke, who in his account in Acts reduces the tensions between the two groups to a dispute about support for the Hellenists' widows, shows clearly that in the persecution that followed Stephen's death only the "Hellenists" had to escape from Jerusalem because only they were beginning to break their ties with the religious community of Judaism. It was indeed no accident that the community which grew out of the "Hellenists'" mission in Antioch was distinguished from the Jews by the name "Christians" (Acts 11. 26).

Almost from the start, the Church existed in different groups, which in the terminology of the period could be quite properly referred to as different *haireseis*, since they were based on different *dogmata*.[5] It was inevitab!e that the seed of Jesus' life should produce different fruit in the soil of the traditional Judaism of Palestine and in the Hellenistic Judaism which had spread in the Diaspora. The faith in Christ which held the groups together had to be more clearly and authoritatively expressed as the boundaries of the religious community of Judaism were left behind, questioned and finally rejected.

II. JERUSALEM AND ANTIOCH

The division into groups which was visible from the start in

---

[4] M. Hengel, "Die Ursprünge der christlichen Mission", *New Testament Studies* 18 (1971/1972), pp. 28 f.
[5] Cf. note 2.

the primitive community took on a clearer form after the expulsion of the Hellenists from Jerusalem. The immediate cause was the development by the expelled group of a very successful mission and their simultaneous abandonment of the mission to the Jews in favour of a mission to the Gentiles and the formation of communities including both circumcised Jewish Christians and uncircumcised Gentile Christians. The missionaries to the Gentiles, whose centre was Antioch in Syria, abandoned the Jewish insistence on circumcision and with it an observance of the law.

The events which made the Apostolic Council and the agreement between the Jerusalem party and the Antiochenes necessary arose out of the growing apart of two Christian groups centred on Jerusalem and Antioch. The first, purely Jewish Christian, observed the Torah and called for observance of the law. The second regarded the law as superseded in Christ and carried out a mission to the Gentiles which ignored the law. In Acts 15 Luke pinpointed the object of the conflict between the groups which was provisionally resolved in Jerusalem. The central question was whether circumcision, and so the law, was necessary for salvation, which involved the question whether the Church of Jesus Christ ought to remain a Jewish Christian Church or not: "But some men came down from Judaea and were teaching the brethren, 'Unless you are circumcised according to the custom of Moses, you cannot be saved.' And . . . Paul and Barnabas had no small dissension and debate with them" (Acts 15. 1–2).

It is important to realize the crucial nature in the Jewish or Jewish Christian view of the problem which divided the two groups. Circumcision was the sign of God's covenant with the chosen people (Gen. 17. 7–11). All the "uncircumcised" were regarded as unclean, they were to be avoided; all fellowship with them was wrong. "Uncircumcised" was a term of abuse. According to Jewish Christian exegesis, Jesus did not come to abolish the law, but to fulfil it (Mt. 5. 17). How could circumcision be abandoned in the mission to the Gentiles?

It became clear in the dispute at Antioch that the agreement reached in Jerusalem, about which we have detailed information from Paul (Gal. 2), had neither fully settled the theological differences nor sufficiently clearly demarcated the complex claims to authority in the carefully separated spheres of the mission to the Jews and the mission to the Gentiles. One point which was agreed between the groups was that observance of the law "should no longer be a criterion for Christianity as a whole",[6] though the agreement resulted in further distinctions between stricter (James) and more liberal (Peter) Jewish Christians and communities willing to compromise (James's formula in Antioch) and the uncompromising apostle Paul. Paul left Antioch, and from now on carried on his missionary work on his own responsibility in Asia Minor and Greece, where he became involved in new disputes with other missionaries and groups in his communities. Again in these new areas, though in a different setting, the question was discussed whether important elements of the Jewish tradition were to claim permanent binding force. In Paul's communities old and new groups joined the discussion. Normally we distinguish between the "parties" in the Corinth community and Paul's "opponents".

III. Parties in Corinth?

In 1 Corinthians Paul appeals to the community in Corinth to agree and not to allow dissensions (*schismata*, 1. 10) to arise among them. Paul has heard of "quarrelling" (*erides*, 1. 11), not personal quarrels among the brethren but the formation of divisive groups in the community which attach themselves to different "party leaders". "Is Christ divided?" he is forced to ask. Scholars have so far been unable to produce a more detailed picture of the individual "parties" in the Corinth community, and that may be because they have concentrated their efforts in the wrong direction, and although the various groups used the names of Cephas, Apollos, Paul and Christ they were still going in the same general direction, and this unity prevented the breakup of the community. According to H. Conzelmann, "Leaving aside all the attempts to give detailed descriptions, one point may be regarded as certain. In the Corinth community there clearly existed a pneumatic, enthusiastic and individualist tendency, but this phenomenon should be seen as operating in the existence of

[6] H. Köster, *op. cit.*, p. 166.

parties itself rather than in the characteristics of individual groups. About these we know nothing. The assumption that the Peter group rejected Paul, for example, is not based on evidence. It should be noted that Paul did not fight against Peter and his party, but against all parties. The same applies to the Apollos group."[7]

The different groups grew up in an environment of Hellenistic Jewish wisdom doctrine, which may have been introduced by Apollos and which led to the development of a pneumatic exaltation christology and, by means of experiences and demonstrations of the spirit and wisdom, to a correspondingly individualistic and clique-based religion. The reception given to Paul's missionary preaching, with its emphasis on eschatology, in the atmosphere of an enthusiasm which celebrated the present possession of wisdom and knowledge as perfection produced a weakening of the zeal Paul expected for the building up of the community as one body, the body of Christ. There were no theological parties in Corinth, only an individualistic theology which divided the community into parties.

IV. PAUL'S OPPONENTS

In 2 Corinthians, Galatians and Philippians Paul attacks groups of missionaries who were spreading "Judaizing" (that is, Jewish Christian) propaganda in the mission territory in which he had worked, in his communities. The main point of their message was a call for a spiritual renewal of the Old Testament law as God's cosmic lordship, and this led them to call for the performance of rites such as circumcision and sabbath observance. Among these missionaries' attractive features were their allegorical interpretations of the Torah, their consciousness of perfection in the spirit which followed from their *"theios-anēr"* christology, their demonstrations of power and brilliant rhetoric. They have been most recently described by J. Gnilka, drawing on the references to them in 2 Corinthians and Philippians. According to Gnilka,

"(a) They fall into the class of universalist trends in contem-

[7] H. Conzelmann, *Der erste Brief an die Korinther* (Göttingen, 1969), p. 48.

porary Judaism, of which they introduced a new variety by their preaching of Christ.

"(b) They preached Christ as the *theios anēr*, a continuation of the line of ancient heroes, from before Moses, whose *dynamis*, which was made over to him in his earthly state, is accessible by virtue of the *Pneuma* which has entered the tradition. The removal of the division between the earthly Jesus and the heavenly Christ made the scandal of the cross superfluous.

"(c) By attaching themselves to the fate of the *theios anēr*, his successors are enabled to overcome the *morphē thanatou* of earthly life and acquire the transforming *dynamis* of Christ.

"(d) Christ's *dynamis* makes itself visible in an exalted consciousness of life and an impressive appearance. Suffering and pain discredit a messenger and his message; this is the specifically anti-Pauline character of these opponents.

"(e) As the perfect, they impart true knowledge by means of a traditional allegorical interpretation of the Scriptures (the law?)."[8]

Paul refuses to recognize the "different gospel" preached by these groups (Gal. 1. 6; 2. Cor. 11. 4 = another Jesus, a different spirit) as the gospel of salvation. Anyone who turns to a "'different gospel', which does not exist, does not go astray in the search for truth, but ultimately sacrifices the search for truth to a lie, which the Galatians believe to have real power because it conceals the 'beings that by nature are no gods', the 'elemental spirits' (Gal. 4. 8). That is why in this case Paul will accept no compromise, only a 'no', no discussion, but only anathema. The truth and reality of the gospel can certainly be given different interpretations—Pauline, Lucan, Johannine, etc. —but it cannot be divided."[9]

In Paul's eyes his opponents are not groups or parties within

---

[8] J. Gnilka, *Der Philipperbrief* (Freiburg, 1968), p. 218.

[9] E. Grässer, "Das eine Evangelium. Hermeneutische Erwägungen zu Gal. 1, 6–10", *Zeitschrift für Theologie und Kirche* 66 (1969), p. 342; H. D. Betz, *Der Apostel Paulus und sie sokratische Tradition. Eine exegetische Untersuchung zu seiner "Apologie" 2 Korinther 10–13* (Tübingen, 1972), p. 42: "Paul is defending himself before the community against the reflections cast by his opponents on his apostolic office. He gives a detailed answer to each of their charges, but addresses the community, not his opponents, for with them no discussion is possible."

the Church, but "heretics", "enemies of the cross of Christ" (Phil. 3. 18). The Christianity growing up in Paul's mission territory increasingly faces a new problem, the problem of heresy. In his fight against "a different gospel" Paul, who proclaimed the gospel as "the power of God for salvation to everyone who has faith, to the Jew first and also to the Greek" (Rom. 1. 16), exposed heresy as "the uncritical extension of an existing language, whether of 'Christian' or 'secular' origin, as a flight into tradition".[10] The heretical party shuts itself up in its language; it rejects communication and therefore faith.

V. CHRISTIAN PARTIES AND GROUPS IN THE CHURCH

After Paul many groups in the Church opposed Christian parties which they rejected as heretics. In Colossians a disciple of Paul's criticizes "Judaizing" Christians, and the author of Revelation mentions as opponents the "Nicolaitans" (Rev. 2. 6, 15), who claim to be Jews but are not (Rev. 2. 9; 3. 9), follow their own "teaching" (Rev. 2. 14, 20) and have mystical knowledge of "the deep things of Satan" (Rev. 2. 24). Ignatius of Antioch also warns against similar heretical Christian groups which have their own methods of biblical exegesis (Phil. 8) and insist on observance of the Old Testament ritual law (Magn. 8; Phil. 6 ff.). The author of 2 John warns against "deceivers ... who will not acknowledge the coming of Jesus Christ in the flesh" (2 Jn. 7; cf. 1 Jn. 4. 2 ff.).

The genuinely Christian groups in the various areas also take shape—partly in such disputes—from their theologies and community structures and from the emergence of their group identities (e.g., the gospel of Matthew, the letters of John and Revelation) and "exclusiveness".[11] From the very beginning, Church

[10] H. Köster, "Häretiker im Urchristentum als theologisches Problem", in E. Dinkler (ed.), *Zeit und Geschichte. Dankgabe an R. Bultmann* (Tübingen, 1964), p. 76.

[11] G. W. Buchanan, *The Consequences of the Covenant (Nov. Test. Supplem.* XX, Leiden, 1970). In chapter 7 of his study, entitled "Covenantal Sectarianism" (pp. 238–81), Buchanan describes, as well as the Jewish "sects", "The Sect of St Matthew" (pp. 272–5), "The Sect of the Johannine Epistles" (pp. 276–9) and "The Sect of the Apocalypse" (pp. 280 ff.). He comments: "The differences between the beliefs and practices of these Christian sects and the Pauline Christians show that Christianity, like Judaism, began with divisions. In neither tradition has there ever been one

unity was a problem of communication between Christian groups, the mediation of theological traditions, compromise on structure and quarrels over the "rule of faith", which was not the possession of any one group but a dynamic criterion closely related to Christian practice. Part of the problem of "Christian groups" from the beginning was also "the experience of different levels within the Christian communities",[12] the juxtaposition of strong and weak, of perfect and fleshly, those who can take "milk" and those who can take "solid food" (Rom., 1 Cor., Heb.), the mixture of simple faithful and trained theologians, of popular piety and theology. The New Testament writers recognized no "class barriers" (N. Brox) which permitted parties, but accepted groupings which were a pressure for solidarity and the demonstration of Christian love.

VI. THE NEW TESTAMENT CHURCH

The New Testament Church took shape as a group within Judaism (the primitive "Hebrew" community) which, in the continuation of the missionary work of Jesus, had an obligation to the whole chosen people of the covenant, which it represented by the college of the "Twelve" (cf. Mt. 19. 28). With the transition to the Gentile mission the Church took on an obligation to "all nations" (cf. Mt. 28. 19) and naturally began to exist in a variety of groups with a variety of geographical situations and religious and cultural inheritances. The Jewish Christians of Palestine, still bound by the law, Hellenistically educated Jews from the Diaspora, receptive to more strongly universalist trends, first in Jerusalem and then in many parts of the ancient Mediter-

---

indivisible community of believers. Sectarianism that began in antiquity continued over into NT times, where it was there also related to purity laws. With this many sects of the same nature it will be possible to note three general sectarian practices, namely: initiation, 'love' and excommunication" (p. 231). The community which lies behind the gospel of Matthew appears to be wrongly described owing to a neglect of tradition criticism, but this suggestive study nevertheless deserves attention in this context. I owe this reference and many other valuable suggestions, to my colleague O. Kaiser of Freiburg.

[12] N. Brox, "Der einfache Glaube und die Theologie. Zur altkirchlichen Geschichte eines Dauerproblems", *Kairos* 14 (1972), p. 163.

ranean world, Gentile Christians who came to the Christian movement through the synagogue and were converted by specifically Christian missionary work: all these made up, sometimes separately, sometimes together, Christian communities whose gradually crystallizing consciousness regarded their "unity" as already given in their one God, their one Lord Jesus Christ, the one Holy Spirit, one baptism and one Lord's supper. "The tensions between Jewish Christian and Hellenistic communities, between Paul and the Corinthian enthusiasts, between John and early Catholicism, were no less than our own. One-sidedness, rigidity, invention and contradictory positions on doctrine organization and piety take up just as much space in New Testament ecclesiology as in modern. . . . The unity of the Church was, is and remains primarily an eschatological state of affairs, something which can only be possessed in so far as it is received as a gift. Church unity can be won only by the faith which hears the voice of the one shepherd and obeys his call to be one flock, his flock."[13] The unity of the Church is lastly the eschatological "state of affairs" of the one love of Christians (Jn. 17), of the lasting eschatological gift (1 Cor. 13) which proves faith to be true faith and guarantees the one lasting hope as true hope.

The existence of the Church in many different communities, the existence of groups, wings, movements and tendencies, theologies, popular devotions and the rest in parishes and church associations, is the result of the preaching of the gospel among all nations, the passing on of the faith to all men and the commitment of many to the one Church. The only side a Christian can take is the side of the Lord and the one Church, his body, which is not divided but lives as many members. Party spirit in the Church can only mean commitment to unity, to communication, to mediation between traditions, to mission, to the building up of the community. Paul described Christian party spirit once and for all: "For though I am free from all men, I have made myself a slave to all, that I might win the more. To the Jews I became as a Jew, in order to win Jews; to those under the law I became as one under the law—though not being myself under

---

[13] E. Käsemann, "Einheit und Vielfalt in der neutestamentlichen Lehre von der Kirche", in *Exegetische Versuche und Besinnungen* II (Göttingen, 1964), p. 266.

the law—that I might win those under the law. To those outside the law I became as one outside the law—not being without law towards God but under the law of Christ—that I might win those outside the law. To the weak I became weak, that I might win the weak. I have become all things to all men, that I might by all means save some. I do it all for the sake of the gospel" (1 Cor. 9. 19–23a). This sort of party spirit, however, leads to anything but the formation of parties, if parties are assumed to be by definition exclusivist. Nor does this sort of party spirit mean the end of "testing spirits" or of the indivisibility of truth; Paul as its apostolic champion is a guarantee of this. It may produce clearly distinct groups, but it will not split them into parties. It may promote pluralism in the Church, but it will not destroy unity. It will promote toleration within the Church, but will be no obstacle to the excommunication of those who reject communication with the Church. In the spirit of Jesus, this sort of party feeling will take the sinner's part, the part of mankind, and only in this way take its own part, because God had mercy on us sinners and took our part.[14]

Translated by Francis McDonagh

[14] Further writing on the subject: W. Bauer, *Rechtgläubigkeit und Ketzerei im ältesten Christentum*, 2nd edn. with postscript by G. Strecker (*Beiträge zur Hist. Theol.* 10, Tübingen, 1964); II. Köster and J. M. Robinson, *Entwicklungslinien durch die Welt des frühen Christentums* (Tübingen, 1971).

Hermann-Josef Vogt

Parties in the History of the Church: Athanasius and his Contemporaries

IN THE history of the Church probably every period exhibits different and even opposing currents, tendencies and groupings, and in some periods they are the most obvious features. Such groupings have been based on theology, church politics and spirituality. They have seen themselves as contributing to the wonderful variety of the one Church, and they have also fought hard with each other and finally led to the formation of sects and to schisms in the Church. From the very beginning there have been groups which became famous for maintaining such a hard line on a particular point that they gradually moved or were pushed out of the Church. In the first century there were the Jewish Christian Ebionites, in the second a variety of gnostic tendencies and the Montanists, with their emphasis on apocalyptic and prophecy. The third century had the purist Novatians, and the fifth the Nestorians and Eutychians respectively supporters of separatist and fusionist christologies.

However, if there is one period of the early Church marked out beyond all others by party struggles, it is the fourth century, and especially the six decades from around A.D. 320 to 380. In this period not only were there groups distinguished by particular theologies, but the episcopate itself was divided into groups which changed from time to time. These groups were very close to parties in the modern sense, and lacked none of the elements which go to characterize a modern party: hard fighting for important positions, vast quantities of propaganda material, a rapid succession of new platforms and statements of principle, efforts

37

to build interest groups, attacks on rivals and constantly changing efforts to form coalitions. The fourth-century parties kept up recruitment by filling episcopal sees which fell (or were made) vacant with clerics of their own persuasion or theology. In the course of this they suffered setbacks, and won victories which were rapidly reversed. What is perhaps the unique feature of this century is the fact that in the end a division in the Church was avoided, and no noteworthy group broke away. (The Arian churches among the Germanic tribes were not breakaway groups from the imperial Church, but completely new bodies which came into existence on its fringe; they accepted the creed supported by the Eastern Roman Emperor in 370 and only the Germanic migrations brought them on to imperial territory, where they died out.

I. THE MOST IMPORTANT GROUPINGS

The most important groupings are familiar to those with only a superficial knowledge of Church history. Around 320, when the division into "left" and "right" is appropriate, there were, on the far left, Arius, who regarded the Son of God as a (spiritual) creation who had a beginning, before which he did not exist, came into being out of nothing, and served the Father only for the creation and government of the world. Opposed to him was his bishop, Alexander of Alexandria, in whose view God had never been without his Son, i.e., his rational word, his wisdom. This position was confirmed in 325 by the Council of Nicaea, which condemned Arius and his principal theses and described the Son as identical to the Father in substance (*homoousios*). For many council Fathers, however, this statement was not a reaction from the centre of the faith against an extreme (left) position, but itself an extreme right view. They signed the formula, but were happy to be allowed after only a few years to ignore it, since behind it they saw the spectre of Sabellianism, the doctrine of one God, which recognized only one divine person active at various times in various masks or roles, as Father, Son or Spirit. This suspicion was very soon strengthened when Marcellus of Ancyra, the earliest (and a very aggressive) defender of the Nicene settlement, produced a concept of God which appeared to be only economically trinitarian; it distinguished Son and

Spirit from the Father in the work of salvation, but openly merged them again with the Father at the end. In this way a broad middle party was formed, which condemned Arius but did not acknowledge the homoousion, though it was prepared to speak of a likeness between Father and Son.

There was an extreme left party, the neo-Arians, who held that the essence of God was his being unbegotten, and that of the Son being begotten, and so found a clear dissimilarity between the two. But this group can be omitted from subsequent discussion because their influence on the course of events was at most negative, even though they made an impression for a time by their skill in disputation. More important were the gradations within the middle party, which ranged from recognition of mere "likeness according to Scripture", through a neutral "likeness in all things", to "likeness in substance" (*homoiousios*), which was no longer very far in meaning from Nicaea, and gave both Hilary and Athanasius a basis for their efforts at reconciliation.

Fascinating though the development of this middle party may be for the historian, it will not be described here, since this party did not produce much of permanent value, except for forcing the defenders of Nicaea to distinguish between substance and hypostasis, concepts which helped the neo-Nicene party (chiefly the three great Cappadocians, Basil the Great, his brother Gregory of Nyssa and his friend Gregory Nazianzen) to find lasting formulas in which to clothe the mystery of the Trinity.

II. The Leading Figures

A short typology of ecclesiastical champions may be of value. I shall take a cross-section through a particularly crucial period: the years around 360, when the "Arianizing" tendency reached its climax towards the end of the reign of Constantius, only to be abruptly reversed with the accession of Julian, now again a pagan, when the process which led to the definitive formulation of the dogma of the Trinity was set in motion, chiefly by Athanasius.

Some other figures may be mentioned: Hilary of Poitiers spent the years 356–60 in exile in the East, but for him the experience was not just a punishment, as it was for some of his companions, but made him a mediator between East and West. Basil of Ancyra made strenuous efforts in theology, but was always one step behind events. Acacius of Caesarea in Palestine was always at least one step ahead of any turn in ecclesiastical politics, and aroused much suspicion as a result. Meletius of Antioch, like Athanasius, was forced into exile three times. Lastly, Lucifer of Calaris was turned into a sectarian by his strident and uncompromising orthodoxy.

Hilary, overshadowed for posterity by the towering Augustine, demonstrated his ability sufficiently by writing the first large-scale Latin work on the Trinity during the four years of his exile. His main interest, however, was the reconciliation of the parties in the Church on the basis of the Nicene formula, which until the time of his exile he had never heard of, but in which he found his inherited faith expressed. This discovery prompted him to write his great letter about the synods or the faith of the East (*Patrologia Latina* 10. 479–548). Here he sometimes sacrifices logic to conciliation, as, for example, when, in order to overcome the Gauls' mistrust of the East and to win Basil of Ancyra and his supporters for Nicaea, he says that the likeness between Father and Son, which Basil's party supported (*homoiousios*), was inconceivable without identity of nature: likeness must mean identity, since things which are unlike cannot be identical (col. 527C). Hilary's positive effect is more a matter of presumption than of demonstration; that he drew a rebuke from Lucifer, he tells us himself in an appendix in which he defends his ever having mentioned the homoiousion (col. 547B).

Basil of Ancyra and his friends took until 358 (when the second Sirmian formula forbade any dogmatic discussion of God and proscribed both *homoousios* and *homoiousios*) to realize that this was more than a linguistic rule, and certainly not a pious principle with support from the Bible, which knew neither expression, but a cover under which implicitly, and thus all the more insidiously, the opinion could spread that the Son was not like the Father in essence, but at the most in his will (cf. Epiphanius, *Panarion haeres.* 73. 15, 1), which made him no more than a perfectly obedient creature. Basil and his friends were ready to defend his divinity, however, and argued the point with Acacius in 369 in Seleucia, only to be finally outwitted by him in Constantinople.

There is a strong sense of men left behind by events in their letter of 363 to the new emperor, Jovian. They proposed to the emperor that either the decisions of Seleucia and Rimini should stand and that any other arrangements should be annulled in the meantime, or that the situation which existed in the Church before the synods should be restored, and bishops everywhere should have the right to meet without the interference of the laity. No one should be allowed, by individual initiatives or deceitful manoeuvres, to introduce general rules, as under Constantius (Sozomenus, *Hist. eccl.* 6. 4). This demand for general freedom of discussion and combination for bishops was totally unrealistic. It was true that the state's interest in the Church as a unifying factor had been the cause of much violence and persecution in previous years, but there were more than practical difficulties in the way of its elimination, since probably none of the Church leaders of the time wanted such a new separation of Church and state.

Acacius, the successor of the learned Eusebius in the see of Caesarea in Palestine, makes a quite different impression. He came to the synod of Seleucia with his own creed already prepared, in which he took up a position to the left of the bishops at the synod, but very close to the views of the emperor, Constantine. By trickery he made sure that his creed was read out. In it he rejected both *homoousios* and *homoiousios* as unscriptural, condemned the assertion of dissimilarity between Father and Son, and taught their similarity with an appeal to Col. 1. 15 ("He is the image of the invisible God"). It evidently escaped the attention of his colleagues that the Son was thus proclaimed visible in substance and therefore of a completely different sort from the Father; but they forced Acacius to admit in the course of discussion that the Son was like the Father only in will, not in substance. He was reminded that this contradicted what he had previously written, but he insisted that no one had ever been judged by his writings alone. He was declared deposed, but went as a delegate of the synod to visit the emperor at Constantinople, where his suggestion prevailed. He was helped by the statement of the Western Fathers, who had completely lost their footing on the theological ice at Rimini (Socrates, *Hist. eccl.* 2, 40). Three years later, however, in company with others, including Meletius, he announced that he accepted and fully supported the creed of Nicaea (Sozomenus, *Hist. eccl.* 6. 4, 7 ff.). From being a long way to the left of Basil of Ancyra in 359, he now left him far behind on the right. At the same time, however, he interpreted *homoousios* as meaning that the Son originated from the substance of the Father and was like him in substance (*ibid.*), which was a return to the views he had held before Seleucia, in opposition to the Nicene formula. It can hardly be held against Athanasius and others that they regarded such adaptability as pure trickery (cf. *Patrol. Graec.* 28, 85 f.).

In his last move, Acacius had allied himself with Meletius, who was as a result also compromised. Meletius deserves to be judged differently from the bishop of Caesarea, however, and not only because Basil the Great was later his firm defender. In 360, having been unable to take up his appointment to the see of Sebaste in Armenia, for which he had been consecrated, Meletius was enthroned in Antioch, since the powerful Acacius and his party regarded him as a supporter. But within a month Meletius had distanced himself. In his first sermon, though he did not mention substance, he defended the divinity of the Son (cf. Epiphanius, *Panar. haer.* 73, 29-33), and he restored many of the clergy who had been removed by his Arian predecessor. The distance between him and his patrons was clear, and before the month was over Meletius was once more deposed and sent into exile. Nevertheless, in the short time in which he had exercised his office, he had succeeded in winning the affection of a majority of the Nicene supporters in Antioch, and from that point he was regarded by the overwhelming majority of the orthodox East as the rightful bishop of Antioch. Meletius was probably not unaware of the expectations attached to him or of the consequences of his behaviour. He is best understood as a man who puts the cause he serves above personal ties and obligations. It is perhaps these aspects of his character which explain why, in spite of Basil's pressure, he made no attempt during his exile to get in touch with Athanasius.

Athanasius and Lucifer never recognized him: Athanasius, because in 363, when he had wanted to enter into communion with him in Antioch, Meletius had put him off (cf. Basil the Great, Ep. 85. 2 to Meletius); and Lucifer, because he had resolved never again to recognize as a bishop anyone who had never defended the Nicene formula. In 362, instead of accepting Athanasius' invitation to a synod at Alexandria, which was to settle the Antioch dispute by finding a way to end the schism between the few un-compromising "Old Nicaeans" and the majority of the Church which accepted Meletius, he went to Antioch himself and there summarily ordained the "Old Nicene" presbyter Paulinus bishop, thus making Athanasius' attempts at reconciliation hopeless in advance (Theodoret, *Hist. eccl.* 3, 5).

III. ATHANASIUS

The great champion of the Nicene settlement, who became a legend in his own lifetime, not only firmly exposed and fought every falling away from the faith of the Fathers of Nicaea (though himself using the word *homoousios* relatively infre-quently), but immediately noticed and tried to encourage every movement in the direction of Nicaea. In his great letter of 359 about the synods of Rimini and Seleucia (ch. 41) he wrote that the term *homoiousios* used by Basil of Ancyra and his friends was also capable of a correct interpretation. It contained, he argued, part of what was meant by *homoousios*, the coincidence in substance between Father and Son; all that had to be added was a reference to the Son's origin from the Father, which was included in the Nicene term. On this point Athanasius' view was clearer than Hilary's. The great monument to Athanasius' policy of reconciliation is, however, the so-called *tomus ad Antiochien-ses*, the document produced by the synod called by Athanasius in 362 after his return under Julian. Among the participants in this synod, apart from the Egyptians, who were friendly to Athanasius, were a number of exiles, including the Westerner Eusebius of Vercelli. Eusebius is mentioned with Lucifer and three other bishops as an addressee of the letter, i.e., as one of those who was to bring about unity in Antioch by implementing the synod's programme, but he is also among the signatories of the letter, and his detailed confirmation of the decisions of the synod, originally in Latin, is also added in Greek translation.

The document begins by remarking that many who were divided only by the disputes (i.e., who were not themselves Arians) now wanted peace with the supporters of Nicaea, and says that everything should be done to encourage this existing trend (ch. 1). No one must be frightened off, but there must nevertheless be a standard by which the newly won orthodoxy can be measured, and this is the Nicene formula: this must be explicitly accepted. But Athanasius realizes that the discussion on God has advanced since Nicaea, making the text of Nicaea by itself unsatisfactory; for example, it says nothing about the sub-stance of the Holy Spirit. For this reason, says the document, there should be added to the Nicene formula a condemnation of those who hold the Holy Spirit to be a creature and separate in substance from Christ. Arius' teaching is only really defeated when no element of the Trinity is called a creature (ch. 2). There is then a summary of the situation in Antioch in which the two groups to be reconciled are described as Paulinus' group and those who celebrate the liturgy in the Old Church (chap. 3). One asks why Paulinus is mentioned when he was no more than a presbyter ministering to his small community, while the large community in the Old Church is treated as a flock without a shepherd, although Athanasius must have known that Meletius, like himself, had returned from exile. When Meletius saw the letter he must have got the impression that Athanasius' attempt to create unity in Antioch by-passed him. This may be the reason why he was not immediately willing, six months later, to enter into communion with Athanasius when he was paying his re-spects to the new emperor, Jovian, in Antioch.

The differences now involved not just acceptance or rejection of the *homoousios* but also, equally strongly, the understanding of the two terms *hypostasis* and *ousia*. At Nicaea they had been treated, without much interest, as more or less equivalent, not, it is true, in the creed itself, but in the appended anathemas: "If anyone says that the Son is of a different hypostasis or *ousia* (from the Father), let him be anathema" (Denzinger–Schönmetzer 126).

This, however, was certainly not a definition of the equivalence. In 341, in the "second formula" of the synod of Antioch, the so-called middle party, for whose credal formulas Hilary showed so much sympathy, had already described the Son as the image of the divinity and *ousia* of the Father, at the same time saying quite plainly that Father, Son and Spirit were three *hypostaseis*, but united in their agreement (*symphonia*: Athanasius, *de syn.* 23. 3 and 6). This sounded like merely moral, rather than substantial, unity and in the West, where *hypostasis* and *ousia* were both translated by *substantia*, the three-hypostasis doctrine was regarded as simply belief in three gods. As such it was attacked at the synod of Sardica in 343, and an attempt was made to present the doctrine of the one hypostasis of Father, Son and Spirit as part of the traditional catholic and apostolic faith. Theodoret, in his history of the Church (2. 8), preserves a dogmatic section of the Sardican circular omitted by Athanasius when he discusses the synod or Sardica in his second apology (ch. 47). This document seems, however, to have been in circulation in 362 and to have provided overzealous Nicenes with a basis for heavy demands on Easterners who wanted peace. For this reason Athanasius bitterly attacked it as representing only a hasty desire for dogmatization on the part of some members of the synod which the synod had reluctantly rejected on the grounds that the Nicene formula could not be altered and needed no revision (*tom. ad Antioch.* 5).

In Athanasius' view it was impossible to rely on Sardica for arguments against the three-hypostasis doctrine, which had to be examined to see what it was trying to say. This was done with great patience by the synod of 362, where the question was asked whether the doctrine should be taken to imply that Father, Son and Spirit should be regarded as differing as creatures or human beings differ, or was an assertion that they were different *ousiai* ("essences" or "substances" in the sense of "stuffs") like gold, silver and bronze, or different gods. The supporters of the three-hypostasis doctrine firmly rejected such interpretations, and explained that the three-hypostasis terminology was intended only to emphasize that Father, Son and Spirit were not just empty names, but denoted realities (*ibid.*).

In exactly the same way, however, the defenders of the one-hypostasis doctrine were also asked whether they, with Sabellius, wanted to reject the Son and the Spirit or deny them substance and reality. The supporters of the one-hypostasis doctrine firmly rejected this idea. They explained their choice of language by saying that for them *hypostasis* and *ousia* had the same meaning, and they talked of one *hypostasis* because the Son is from the *ousia* of the Father and the (divine) nature (*physis*) in them is the same (ch. 6). The synod's document then records that both groups recognized the terminology of the other as possible and legitimate, and agreed not to accuse each other on account of differences of language, but only to require each other to recognize the Nicene formula and the condemnation of the old errors, such as those of Sabellius and the Gnostics.

There was, of course, already agreement on the condemnation of the Arians. The reason for the specific mention of the Gnostics here is that Eastern theologians always suspected that the one-hypostasis doctrine concealed a materialistic image of God: a God who developed into a Trinity by extension or emanation. This agreement, of course, did not come about over the opposition, or even against the will, of Athanasius, which means that Athanasius accepted in principle the three-hypostasis doctrine. This is all the more amazing because he maintained even after 362 the identification of *ousia* and *hypostasis* which had been associated with him since the beginning of the Arian struggle.

In 369, in a letter to the African bishops, he said "*Hypostasis* is *ousia* and has no other meaning than being itself; . . . *hypostasis* and *ousia* is (*sic*) existence" (*hyparxis*: PG 26, 1036B). But it is perhaps even more amazing that in 362 Athanasius did not simply accept without examination the doctrine of those who used the same terminology as himself, but had them carefully questioned to see whether it did not conceal Sabellianism, the doctrine of one person. In this Athanasius could be a model for all times. Every theologian must be capable of understanding formulas which use a different language from his own and accepting them as legitimate; even more important, he must be on his guard against regarding his own terminology as irrefutable to such an extent that those who use it are automatically regarded as orthodox. If this second feature of Athanasius' practice had been taken seriously as a model, it would have prevented many unfortunate incidents in Church history; it would, for example, have kept his third successor, Cyril, from uncritically adopting Apollinarian formulas which were declared to be Athanasian. Perhaps we still have something to learn from Athanasius today, when we have got as far as learning to be critical of the past. Groupings could be as valuable in the future as in the time of Athanasius in contributing to a broader understanding of the truth, provided they were not fixed in advance in rigid party attitudes. It is not too much to say that in this respect, without changing his own habits of thought, Athanasius opened the way for the conceptual development which had already begun in the East (cf. Epiphanius, *Panar. haer.* 73, 16) and which later enabled the three great Cappadocians to reformulate the mystery of the Trinity in accurate language. If the Old Nicene identification of *ousia* and *hypostasis* had been retained, neither the theology of the Trinity nor the christology of the next century would have been put into theologically defensible definitions. The terminology of those whom Epiphanius as late as the mid-370s was still describing as Semi-Arians was in this way not only tolerated throughout the Church, but even became the official terminology of the councils. The direction of this development was fixed by Athanasius at his synod in Alexandria in 362.

It is worth noticing in this connection that Athanasius did not plead for either general fraternization or a collective amnesty for abandoned heresies and errors. He made a clear distinction between those who had taken a leading part in the fight against the sense of the Nicene settlement and those who had let themselves be carried along with it by force or moral pressure. The former, if they now honestly accepted the Nicene formula, were accepted into communion but were not allowed to remain in their church offices. Members of the second group were allowed to retain their clerical status. As Athanasius wrote to Rufinian, the bishops in Greece, Gaul and Spain agreed to this. Lucifer of Calaris was the only dissenter.

The synod of 362 also achieved at least one success in christology which went beyond the theology of Athanasius himself and destroyed in advance the basis of an error which was only just beginning to show itself. Athanasius always thought of the incarnate Christ in terms of *logos* and *sarx*, of the divine Logos dwelling and acting in a human body. He does not talk of Christ's having a human soul; the idea would have had no meaning in his system. It was but a short step as from this position to actually denying the existence of a human soul in Christ: one taken by Apollinaris, bishop of Laodicea. Apollinaris admitted a lower (animal) soul in Christ, but held that the true rational soul or highest part of the soul (the *nous*) had been replaced in Christ by the divine Logos. Against this view the synod of 362 declared that the Logos had not assumed a body without a soul (or life), senses or reason (or mind: *anoeton*); he had not won salvation merely for the body, but for the soul as well. The Only-begotten became the Firstborn, and was one and the same Christ who suffered in the flesh and awakened the dead with divine power (*tom. ad Antioch*. ch. 7).

The synod's statement did not prevent the Apollinarians from making use of Athanasius' name and in this way getting Cyril of Alexandria to accept Apollinarian formulas as Athanasian. It would be a great mistake to exaggerate the effect of the synod of 362. At first it had no effect at all because Lucifer of Calaris refused to be associated with it and, before its instructions reached Antioch, had ordained Paulinus as bishop there, and so given the split institutional form. Paulinus, however, seized the opportunity and signed the acts of the synod, and indeed added his own detailed acceptance of them, which, in the crucial passages on the doctrine of the Trinity and christology, agreed word for word with the synod's document (ch. 11). It may have been this which, at the latest after Meletius had snubbed Athanasius in 363, brought him final recognition in Alexandria and so also in Rome. Athanasius did not again alter his attitude to Paulinus and Meletius in the last ten years of his life (363–373), not even after Basil the Great, since 370 bishop of Caesarea in Cappadocia, had appealed to him in a number of highly respectful letters to enter into communion with Meletius himself and persuade the West to do the same. Basil's proposal was that Meletius should be recognized as sole bishop in Antioch and the other groups subordinated to him (Basil, Ep. 66, 67), which would have meant that Paulinus, who had been recognized by Athanasius and the West for over a decade, would have had to take second place. Basil also asked Athanasius to have his friend Marcellus of Ancyra condemned for his Trinitarian errors, which were still an obstacle to the acceptance of Nicaea by many Eastern Churches (Basil, Ep. 98. 2). Marcellus had been Athanasius' comrade in the battle for Nicaea, his companion in exile, and had been rehabilitated with him at Sardica (cf. Athanasius, *2nd Apology* 45. 1).

Basil's request was too much. Though he knew more about him than anyone else, Athanasius never condemned Marcellus.

Even when that great enemy of heretics, Epiphanius, asked him face to face about Marcellus' teaching, he said nothing, but just smiled. Epiphanius believed that by so doing he neither spoke in favour of Marcellus nor rejected him. It is amazing how accurately Epiphanius claims to interpret Athanasius' smile. It means, he says, that Marcellus is not far from evil (heresy), but should be regarded as pardoned (*apologesamenon: Panar. haer.* 72. 4. 4). Marcellus seems to have died in the same year as Athanasius or perhaps a year later (*ibid.* 72. 1. 1). Whether Athanasius would have agreed to a posthumous condemnation of Marcellus we do not know. What is certain, however, is that the history of the Church and of doctrine in the half-century after the death of Athanasius, and indirectly long after, was marked by the fact that the Church of Antioch remained divided, and the really influential community there had no connection with Rome. As a result, Antioch was unable to develop into a church centre on the scale of Alexandria, but had to put up with a supervision from Alexandria based on a Roman commission, or at least good contacts with Rome. The imagination has no limits when one tries to construct what the course of the Nestorian dispute might have been if Antioch had traditionally had good relations with Rome. Would there have been a Monophysite reaction at the council of Chalcedon if Cyril's Roman commission had not made him such a dominant figure?

One conclusion is justifiable. If the strategy of reconciliation planned by Athanasius at the synod of 362 had achieved its intended object instead of being nullified by Lucifer's clumsy hyperorthodoxy, the harvest which had matured in the heat of the theological controversies would have been gathered earlier, and the Eastern Church would have been spared many of the fruitless party struggles of the 370s. Nevertheless, even if this immediate success in ecclesiastical politics was lost, theology and the history of doctrine down to our own day have benefited from the fact that, in spite of his firm position in the party struggles of the fourth century, Athanasius never gave way to blind party spirit, and never lost sight of the issue which lay behind and beyond the disputed formulations.

Translated by Francis McDonagh

Marie-Dominique Chenu

Confrontation without Schism
in the Medieval Church

"'HERESIES': the word has its uses, and has been used much, yet it is as equivocal today as in the medieval Church." That was the opinion of a man who knew the Western Middle Ages as only an expert does—Professor L. Génicot of Louvain.[1] The ambiguity of the word expresses the ambiguity of the situations.

Instead of speculating abstractly on the concepts of heresy, orthodoxy and dogma, I shall look at the facts and the behaviour of the people of God constituted in the Church within the critical period of the twelfth and thirteenth centuries. The Church-in-action is a theological location whose actual density does not, of course, invalidate theoretical criteria, but which marks legal and authoritarian categories with a relativism accordant as much with human social reality as with the truth of the gospel.

I chose that period in Church history (1130–1215) because the transformation that occurred then derived not from a moral reformation by way of authoritarianism, as in the time of Gregory VII, but from an evangelical shock to Christian people in and through their solidarity with an economico-political social development. The gospel revival is homogeneous with a transformation of man. The "connaturalism" (if the term is permissible) of this transformation and this revival gives us, in conjunction with the documents, the objective contexts and subjective criteria of what are known as "heresies".

We then have a trustworthy dossier on a characteristic period,

[1] L. Génicot, Le XIIIe siècle européen (Paris, 1968), p. 266.

which enables us to observe and criticize in pastoral behaviour as in theological pronouncements the trends, tensions, divergences and affinities, critical dissatisfactions, marginalizations, insidious integrationism, suppressed heresies, traditions and resurgences, contagious and aggressive actions and subtle counterpoints which, more or less consciously, were already very different one from the other, and were eventually geared down by the fermentation of cultural, spiritual and intellectual dissensions.

At that time, heresies raged which were explicit, conscious, organized, perceived and denounced as such by the community, by the people and the hierarchs: in the twelfth century, Catharism, with its Manichean dualism backed by an evangelical fervour, not only covered a specific group and area, but also extended its seductive effects beyond its confessional supporters, and benefited from infiltrations into the flock of the faithful.

My task here is not to produce a typology of a heresy as such; however, in order to describe the geography of tensions and frontiers, it is necessary both to observe closely the contaminations which keep them going, and to look closely at this explicit rupture of the unity of the faith. Heresy, at least in its first stage, before becoming a new orthodoxy, was not monolithic, nor was the community which it threatened. Orthodoxy was not monolithic: it was stimulated and impressed as much as threatened by the aspirations and enthusiasms of heresy; and also dominated by the more respectable political options. Were the Ghibellines against the pope in Italy heretics? The Toulousians against the Crusaders of Montfort in France? Arnold of Brescia, who fired the community of Rome against those pontiffs who were turning the gospel into power?

Confrontation in the Church is always ambiguous. Together with unhealthy outbreaks it features healthy reflexes. More than the sociologist, the theologian (if undetached by scholasticism from the Bible) studies with infinite care the shape and course of aspirations and mental attitudes within the "frontiers" of heresy.

My inquiry was inspired by a concern to discern the tendencies and imbalances of faith, and so I shall not trace the chronological series of spiritual and ecclesiastical events, nor their geographical variety. I am concerned with the developments, the neuralgic areas of ambiguities, tensions, dissensions, which encourage internal confrontation, in doctrine, in the institution, and in collective behaviour.

I. POPULAR MOVEMENTS

These standpoints and critical upheavals occurred, in conduct more than in statements, in popular circles: from Etienne de Muret to Francis of Assisi, with Norbert le Prémontré or Pierre Valdès, in Milan and in Lyon, among the Patarins as well as the Umigliati, the new prophets did not address the clerics directly. It is difficult to be exact about the social impact of their message. It affected city folk, burgesses, labourers and the leisured, tramps, cultured nobles; on any hypothesis, among Catholics as well as Cathars, it is untrue to the facts to reduce the troubles to class conflict, since the evangelical ferment made its mark everywhere. What was decisive was the call to a population whose Christian consciousness had been inert until then—an amorphous mass. The Gregorian reform had certainly appealed to the faithful as against unjust and dishonest clergy, but in that very struggle against abuses it tended towards a rehabilitation of the priesthood and proclaimed the role of the priest. The hierarchy was invested not only with the power of government for the common good of Christian society, but with the power of sanctification. Hence there was an increasingly strong division between hierarchy and people, in a "clerical" Church proceeding along an authoritarian path.

This minor group emerged with a more lively consciousness, extended beyond the insignificant local communities, and achieved, by various economic exchanges, an overall solidarity. A human area formed which was amenable to popular movements, but quasi-marginal in relation to the hierarchical frameworks. An anti-clerical mentality developed, sometimes even going so far as to put in question the traditional doctrinal structure, and in particular its sacramental framework, as happened with Pierre Valdo, excommunicated in 1184 and, supported by a pantheist metaphysics, Amaury de Bène († 1206); but more often it was a question of an aggressive resentment which did not lead to any doctrine departing from the Church's teaching.

Henri de Lausanne contested the sacramental efficacy of un-worthy priests and the official marriage morality. Several depre-cated the ossification of monastic virtues. Most accused the Church of not being up to its mission and denounced, sometimes in demagogic terms, its incapacity and unworthiness. The teach-ing of priests was rejected and a summary evangelism adopted. But there was no construction of these tendencies into a dissident theology. Among many popular preachers there was Tanchelm, the guiding spirit of the theocratic community of Anvers (c. 1130), who was accused of the worst errors, but was in fact an unskilled reformer, in his recourse to laymen and women. Odo de Stella († c. 1148), though extravagant, showed more psychological disorder and social upset than heresy, and gave St Bernard a good opportunity to exercise rigid orthodoxy.

II. Socio-economic Conditions

These form the second-line element in this ferment, which began to affect the structures of society and to infect the estab-lished order with its divisions. It is no mean thing to lay oneself open to the accusation of heresy against a religion which had sacralized a providential order. When the frameworks and values of the feudal order lost their primary substantiation, and victimized men instead of supporting them, Christian people, here and there, found themselves supporting insurrections for the sake of liberation. Declarations of freedom were obtained from lords, irrespective of whether the lords were bishops, benefiting from the submission of serfs in their service. In all these cases, the general collusion of the Church with feudal bodies, both in terms of princely alliances and rivalries as well as in economic conditions and administration, was called in question.

In this way the rebellion of the new social classes and the com-position of charters of liberation came up against the complaisant mood of the evangelical movement and the "poor of Christ". The history of the movement is continuous from the winning of independence by the Lombard cities in 1183 by the peace of Leganno (where the "bourgeois" militia were victorious over the emperor) up to the composition of the charter of Bergamo by the Dominican prior Guala, some time around 1230, and that of

Milan (with the assistance of Peter of Verona, himself a Dominican).

The interactions are inextricable, but imply a violation of oaths. The knot sacralizing feudal relations and the basis of the old society was untied. Its value was contested not merely by the development of social relations, but in the name of the gospel. This brought in sanctions, excommunications, accusations of heresy, from the church authorities. This mixture of decadent feudalism and political insurrection compromised the high powers of kings, princes and pontiffs. Hence the barons and rebellious burgesses who rose against King John in England (from whom they obtained Magna Charta, 1215) came under the edict of excommunication of Innocent III, in the course of a long and bitter conflict.

Robert Grosseteste, the bishop of Lincoln, strong in cultural ascendancy as well as in hierarchical power, told his opponent, the Dominican Jean de Saint-Gilles, that he was holding him and his brothers as heretics, and called upon him to apply to himself the formal definition of heresy (which that master of theology seemed to have forgotten).

In fact, by its very etymology, the concept of heresy can be extended beyond religious denominations proper to ideologies, which, though profane in object and reference, include a total commitment of the human being to a cause. Such is a deep and passionate assent to a political idea of the world, even within a strictly unified collectivity. There is a form of totalitarian attachment at the limit point of a process of sacralization, opposed to deviation, which may be taken as a "heresy".

Beneath these political behaviours, the life of the time was committed; it offered a human soil for religious denunciations. With the emancipation of the "bourgeoisie", intensive urbanization won through to an awareness of autonomy and freedom.

It was in the towns that these "innovationists" found their heretical advocates. The town is the written expression (written on soil) of a conception of society: the new towns outside the *feudal* castrum.

The Cistercians had been the leaders of a sensational evolution of agriculture, but St Bernard threatened the towns and their schools. The monk Rupert of Deutz, faced with the growth of the Rhineland towns, remembered that Cain had been the first builder of a town. It was not by accident that Arnold of Brescia († 1155), leading spirit of the Roman revolutionary commune, while contesting a Church of Powers, had been a disciple of Abélard's (himself a superior cultural product of urban civilization).

The universities, true "cultural communes", had won their independence from the political powers (Paris, 1228); they were to become the locations for the new theology, developed by the members of the mendicant Orders—a long way from monastic theology, which was homogeneous with the feudal world.

Jacques de Vitry (a student at Paris, 1187) violently denounced the Communes instead of a heretical pestilence exactly like Etienne de Tournai, then priest of Sainte-Geneviève in Paris (1180), who challenged the vulgarization of theology in the public area; i.e., outside a monastic framework.

In addition, the development of the market economy, fed by the rise of productivity, impossible during the feudal stagnation, gave rise to a mobility of élites, both cultural and business: a mobility assisting the diffusion of heresies within the new economy. There were not only facilities for meetings, exchanges and proselytism exploited by the new apostles in popular debates, but also (and above all) mental attitudes adopted (in the face of rigid ecclesiastical structures) by men used to frequent moves and therefore open to larger vistas. Social dynamism, typical of urban society, actually favours the growth of oppositional attitudes to the stiffening and growing formalism of that increasingly legal mentality which dominated in curial environments and in the greater part of the ecclesiastical hierarchy. That is the sociological explanation of heresies (to the extent that a faith is consistent and is expressed in a culture).

III. Good News for the Poor

Perhaps the name chosen by those suspect prophets is the most revealing thing, ecclesiastically as well as sociologically. They called themselves the "poor of Christ". Evangelical poverty is the mystical and economic spring of this movement. The most significant case is that of Francis of Assisi, not only because of his fierce evangelism, but because of the sociological absolutism of his criterion. He eventually got to the point where his disciples broke up—the spirituals against the conventuals—following on a radicalism with no desire to make peace with the institution, or with clericalization, codification and knowledge.

It was the gospel which was in question. It was wanted in its pure state, as an absolute reference, in its essential text, without any gloss, apart from all rules, whether Benedictine or Augustinian, stressing the intrepid spontaneity of the prophets. The return to the origins, recourse to the primitive life of the community of Jerusalem (Acts 2), the myth of the apostles (*Ordo apostolorum*, one of the sects called themselves), the rejection of the gift of Constantine, for he had compromised the Church: all these are elements of a subversive memory. Direct reading by laymen of the gospel in the vernacular is certainly an occasion to get at the clerics, and a motive for ignoring legalistic observances, but more profoundly and beyond any claims, it was the rediscovery of Christianity, defined as a life, in a rule of incarnation, where Christ was proclaimed as the only Lord, that mattered.

The (not only moral but constitutional) benefit of this announcement of the word of God was brotherhood, the categorical law of the gospel. St Francis was the perfect herald. He recreated the image and vocation of brother. He was among those who were then in the course of changing history. We can see the mystical and apostolical flowering; but we also have to discern the causes of and risks in the economic transformation of society. The increase in techniques, from changing production methods, brought about a psychological traumatism in a world where feudal social relations had held together for four centuries the sacred hierarchy of a kindly paternalism, the ideal of which was to become a man's servant. The work ethic changed—with the taste for initiative and the arrival of plenty—into the effective promotion of man, into horizontal communities. It was not by chance that Francis was the son of a rich Assisi merchant, exactly like Valdo in Lyon. The mendicants were, paradoxically, the confidants and guarantors of the new classes, in an economy of progress and profit.

In this logic of brotherhood (only too quickly subdued by the bourgeois oligarchy of the towns), there disappeared the division of mankind into three *ordines*: *oratores*, *bellatores* and *laboratores*. Adalbéron of Laon had fixed the formula at the time of Hugues Capet, after the year 1000. Christians made up only one body; but society includes three estates: priests, gentlemen and peasants (who held possessions only through suffering, and thanks to whom the religious and military functions were kept going). The general sacralization of society, or the word *ordo*, a religious term, covered the spiritual and the temporal. It disappeared with the rehabilitation of work and the reconstruction of the world. The states of life (*status*) were substituted for the orders, and the new apostles considered the profession of production as a vocation worthy of salvation. The trade corporations were at best *fraternitates*, sworn brotherhoods, including those of the merchants, who until then had been "accursed". They were the perfect clients for the new religious orders, to the annoyance of the traditional parish and monastic clergy. St Bernard exalted the chivalrous ideal, christianizing warlike force for the sake of priestly power. With Francis and his like, the poor are the first to know the mystery of the Kingdom.

The earthly life of Christ, his love, his poverty, his sufferings, polarized the faith and enthusiasm of believers. Of course, God remained the Father, and Francis always called him the All-Powerful. Aquinas built his theological *Summa* on the schema of the Creation—emergence and return. But with the humanization of God and the message of Christ, the reference to the Creator no longer comprised an objective and eternal reality, willed by God, in a providence whose order made a social revolution impossible. Holiness did not consist in accepting with submission this image of the world, but in co-operating in its construction, according to the profane condition of vocation. The Christian economy ran forward into history, and time entered into the object of theology, instead of being merely the absence of eternity. The ambiguity of mental attitudes features a socio-economic and a spiritual confrontation and contestation. Christianity had surrendered its role as the ideology of the feudal regime; and the hierarchy of the Old Testament had ceased to be (by means of allegory) the model of the people of God.

IV. THE RULE OF THE SPIRIT

The reign of the Spirit favoured this revival, these hopes and this messianism. The Golden Age was no longer in the past, and the return to the *vita apostolica* initiated the new creation, in accordance with the promise of Christ in sending the Spirit. The deterioration of the Church was only provocation of an apocalypse, and the prophets announced the imminence of the Kingdom, as Christ himself had announced it. Here was the eleventh hour. On the one hand, all human behaviour, including that of the institutional Church, was relative. On the other hand, the way was open for the consummation of God's plan. This was a legitimate hope, though favouring the illusions of popular millenarianism as well as necessary innovations.

Joachim of Flora systematically expressed these eschatological aspirations, in his conception of the three ages of the history of salvation, and in a foretelling of new prophets who would inaugurate the era of the Spirit. Co-operation with new groups, particularly with the spiritual Franciscans, was decided in advance. History was made at the frontiers of centuries. The time of signs and images was completed: now for the new Church. The eschatological perspective opportunely relativized the legal status of the terrestrial Church and showed it economy in the development of history.

It is pointless to analyse the faith apart from its cultural suasions; similarly, one cannot define heresy without reference to its sociological roots.[2]

Translated by V. Green

[2] Every page and line deserves a bibliographical reference or a bibliographical indication. The reader must refer to experts for more detail: H. Grundmann, for Germany; R. Manselli, R. Morgen, C. Violante, for Italy; E. Delaruelle, M. H. Vicaire, J. LeGoff, Ch. Thouzellier, M. Mollat, for France. But the papers of the international *Heresies and Societies* (Paris, 1968) colloquium should be consulted anyway.

Oreste Kéramé

Pluralism in the One Church: The Apostolic Churches of the East

I. AUTONOMOUS CHURCHES

THERE has always been an Eastern Church within the one Christendom. That is to say, an integral catholicity owing nothing to the Roman primate, or to its atavisms before Christ: neither in its apostolic origin, nor in its theology, nor in its liturgy, nor in the form of its sacraments, nor in its sacramentals, nor in its law, nor in its missionary activities, nor in its attitudes to the "world", to politics, society, the state; to say nothing of its monastic life and spirituality. Yet that was a catholicity existing for centuries in a state of reciprocal life in common with Rome and its effective dependencies in western Europe: with, indeed, the very independent Latino-African churches.

This Eastern Church was one in its original form and in its non-Roman deployment in the unity of reciprocal communion with the West (mainly the papal West), yet diverse in terms of its individual churches, which were multi-apostolic in origin, knew nothing or retained nothing apart from Augustine of Augustinianism.[1] But it has not been without high intellectual quality and prayer, religious thinkers, canonists, liturgists, spiritual writers, mystics and eminent pastors, throughout the centuries, throughout the unique "people of God".

Surely it is not necessary to recall in detail the pre-Augustinian schools of Alexandria and Antioch, their variety, and their con-

---

[1] Apart from a few very subsidiary and delayed accretions, which were indirect and remained doubtful in regard to orthodox sacramental matter.

trary methodological approaches, theological thought, and differences in ecclesiastical policies from their hierarchical authorities.

No historian will be unaware of the "Pharaonic" monarchism of the Church of Egypt, which was more centralist than Rome once was in ancient Italy (its initial and most stable realm of influence), once Milan had been deprived of imperial power. In its Coptic continuation the Egyptian Church maintained its absolute and direct jurisdiction over Ethiopia (in the form of the delegacy of the unique "Abouna") until just before the middle of the present century. In this it contrasts with the quite synodical and canonical aspects of the patriarchal methods of Antioch and Constantinople, the new ecclesiastical Antioch situated on the Bosphorus at the same time as the new imperial Rome. Of course they, like others, exhibited certain tendencies to extend their frontiers or ecclesial attributions.[2]

In fact, from the theological viewpoint, it was Alexandria which, with an Antiochian counterweight in the shape of the Byzantines, was dominant throughout the East, except among the Assyro-Chaldeans of the Persian Empire. This is obvious from the rejection of Chalcedon on the one hand by a large part of the East within the Roman Empire, in Armenia and in Ethiopia, as well as by the Council of Justinian (the fifth ecumenical Council), at which the Chalcedonian Churches of the East reaffirmed their dominant Alexandrian intellectual and devotional tendencies.

This Alexandrian eastern theology was oriented wholly towards the deification of man by the redemptive incarnation. A major instance (not forgetting Clement) of this trend was Origen, a forerunner in dynamic variety of all Christian theologies. But the theological survival of the great Alexandrian is to be found more outside than within Egypt. He was expelled by his bishop as a dangerous influence; he was then supported far from the banks of the Nile by Heraclas, formerly his pupil and then his co-director in the school.

The Alexandrian theology is found in its most orthodox form

---

[2] This was a tendency more obvious in Alexandria, Constantinople and Rome. Antioch above all remained on the defensive, though quite weakly. There was no word from Jerusalem.

in Cappadocia, with which the names of Basil the Great, the two Gregorys (the theologian and the philosopher) are primarily associated. Preceded by Firmilian of Caesarea (the impetuous theological associate of St Cyprian), they were fittingly succeeded (as doctors at least) by Cyril, a geographical Alexandrian and a contemporary of St Augustine. Centuries later this noteworthy succession was completed by Palamas of Athos and Thessalonica, a star in the firmament of ecumenical orthodoxy, and something of a counterpart to Aquinas in the Aristotelian pantheon of Roman scholasticism.

The foregoing summary is intended as a quick rundown of the factual situation in the life of the Church, and notably that before the great schisms (including that still persisting). All the way back to the New and Old Testaments, pluralism is as much a fact as the law of Christian unity.

II. Rejection of the Western Middle Ages

The attention paid by the West, both Catholic and Protestant (owing apostolic origin to primatial Rome, or organized by Rome[3]), to the Christian East was only marginal, it would seem. It saw itself (in fact, if not in principle) in its particular Romano-Augustinian tradition (accepted or discussed in its more Roman elements) as the whole of Christianity. That indicates more an unconscious racism in the Church than a climate of schism. Above all, if a local church bases its claim on gradual accessions of a universal, direct and divinely received sovereign power. That gives rise to a view which is limited in a secular sense (and therefore necessarily erroneous) of Christianity throughout its entire historical existence. Hence pastoral, doctrinal, hierarchical and spiritual distortions leading, by a sheer lack of diverse horizons, to factitious dead-ends.

The seriousness and origin of this misfortune in its more Catholic manifestations are indicated by Yves Congar. "On the intellectual level and on that of social relations, many [contemporary]

[3] There is good reason to take into account a diffuse Eastern evangelization—a Smyrnean one, for instance, among the Gauls—and the originality of the Celtic Church, later Romanized in Britain, and from there in Ireland.

measures are characteristically tantamount to a rejection of the [Western] Middle Ages together with the medieval ontology, historical interpretation of the world and society, devotions and a priesthood with a claim to power.... I am increasingly sure that the break between East and West and then that of the sixteenth century were determined by a rejection of the Western Middle Ages."[4]

It could not be put more appositely. The Western Middle Ages tried to impose on the East in all its apostolic variety. It did not succeed. That is the synthetic explanation of what is known as the "Eastern schism". Or rather, what is worse, it succeeded only miserably, in the shape of Uniatism,[5] that captive of a particular Church conceiving itself (for illusory reasons of a hypertrophied Right) as equivalent to the actual ecclesial Whole—apart from occasional second thoughts with ephemeral or void consequences.

This state of affairs continued throughout the Reformation and modern times right up to ecumenism: an isolation of Catholicism glorying in its fierce determination to maintain its heritage in its medieval form considered as an absolute.[6] Consequently the entire dynamic equilibrium of pluralism and unity in the Church was rendered constantly unstable as far as Catholic perspectives and activities were concerned.

It is not that there were no reactions (authentic signs of vitality) in the Catholic Church, once separated thus, from the time of Gregory VII, from the living tradition of the apostolic East, cut off from its Protestantized elements, self-isolated from a Western environment reconnected by the Renaissance to pre-Christian Hellenism, and discarding all ecclesiality in an increase of laïcism.

[4] *Eprit*, special number 1971, p. 624.

[5] A distress all the greater for being less perceived. What is sadder than a state of euphoria in the midst of depersonalization?

[6] Towards the thirties there was in Paray-le-Monial (perhaps there still is) a "diorama" representing the "triumphs of the Church". It triumphed —visibly—over Arius, Nestorius, Eutyches, Photius, Luther, Calvin and Henry VIII ... and a few others. On emerging, one of my friends at the time (who has since then become a famous theologian but has stayed my friend and is none other than Père de Lubac) said to me: "Another two or three triumphs like that and there won't be anything left." That was the reaction of Vatican II to the "triumphalism" which was then quite obligatory in apologetics.

III. Collegiality

It is reasonable to suppose that the various "Gallican" manifestations which followed on the conciliarism of the sixteenth century (itself related to certain Latin "African" positions of patristic times) were essentially (notably in the shape of the minority-opinion Fathers of Vatican I, but also in the more mature churches) something other than errors of Catholic theology. They intended an exposition of what had to be reaffirmed and rediscovered, at Vatican II: that is, apostolic collegiality surviving in the episcopate. This collegiality is the constitutional basis of pluralism in unity; in relation to it, a doctrinal primacy or a primacy of action is conceivable only when integrated, without that integration destroying collegiality itself. That was the fatal consequence of primacy conceived as congenital to the episcopate seen and expressed as an absolute sovereignty; just as if it had been conceived apart from collegiality, without aboriginal, permanent and ultimate links with collegiality. These were links requiring description and expression in laws—in canons without shades of ambiguity; for there is no question here of eternal truths to be believed in their venerable mystery, but of the exercise of a pastorate of faithfulness and righteousness, of a public ministry in time.

The very legitimacy of this pastorate would be dubious if its exercise showed it as a source of division, of disintegration, or of oppression: in short, of a functional distortion of the supposed purpose of the ministry. In view of my short summary of the monumental fact of the Eastern Church, which by the mere form of its extra-Roman structure requires a fundamental ecclesial understanding of the Church as a whole, and in view of my brief remarks on the collegial currents met with throughout historical Latinism or Catholicism (above all, after the loss of "communion with the East"), certain conclusions now seem possible, which can be summarized thus: in Christianity there are various ways (mainly collective) of thinking and acting without surrendering unity in the Faith; or of behaving in accordance with Christ. There are, in other words, various ways of realizing this unity in living imitation of the trinitarian reality of the one God reflected in men. For the Churches as for the faithful, to be "catholic" is to be "different", as the Father, Son and Spirit differ in the unity of their essence, which is love undying, dynamic relations, truth.

This general conclusion may be illustrated, for instance, in ecumenical relations, and more particularly in the most recent manifestations of Rome–Constantinople ecumenism. You will remember the letter of 8 February 1971 from Paul VI to Athenagoras I, which stated that between the Roman Church and the "Venerable Orthodox Churches", there was virtually full communion, and that there was only a "final step" to be taken before perfect communion.

But there can be no question of adjusting at one go all Catholic-Orthodox differences merely by bringing them together. One calls to mind the "Filioque", the papal primacy of "divine rights", infallibility, original sin, grace, the sacraments in general and each of them in particular, the definitive canonicity of conciliar decisions, Mariology, the possibility of divorce, and so on: differences dating for the most part from before the Schism which in their time did not prevent full communion ... though not, it is true, clouds, storms and tempests.

If there were things requiring improvement in the Latin-Greek pluralism of the time of union, perhaps there is also a possibility of other pluralisms in unity. Here the Mother-Churches of Rome and the East could learn something from Anglicanism and Protestantism, from the non-Christian religions and non-denominational philosophies. That has already occurred to some extent by means of various, inevitable and fruitful "osmoses". For example, there is the debt owed by all Christian Churches to the non-denominational and even anti-clerical philosophical current in social affairs and individual liberty. Or there is the debt owed by Catholic theology to Newman, that Origen of more recent times, by virtue of the tendencies that he awakened (because of his Anglican origins and life, his sense for the best of the Reformation), and for the intellectual and moral mood of "subsequent" times. It is also conceivable that Vatican II would not have wished to be so "pastoral" without any influence from contemporary existentialism.[7]

[7] This was surely what made a young American priest say: "I'd never have thought there were so many bishops who thought like everyone else."

The unity which is in God in his trinity is reflected everywhere in creation. Therefore it is requisite in the Church as actuality. At the level of consciousness and conscience it is provided by faith, hope and charity in the unity of grace, revealing in the different lives of the saints the one Lord Jesus.

Clearly what is primarily asserted in the Augustinian "... *in necessariis unitas"* nowadays concerns the papacy as bond of unity. Ecumenism is a general Christian phenomenon of our times, which also feature an internal crisis in Roman Catholicism. But from these two viewpoints, the same problem is posed in the desire for a new understanding of the papacy as a factor of unity in diversity. We would wish it simultaneously more universal and more limited.

More universal; hence more detached from a living, exclusive, ecclesiastico-social-ethnic-historical, local, Roman, particularly Italian and (*descrescendo*) Latin, European, Western and white image. More limited. Because "... however great [the popes] may be..., they are as us". They have their health, their nerves, their family history, their undying youth, their pre-papal life, and their individual physiologico-psychological make-up. They cannot do everything. The whole life of the Church (and, virtually, that of all mankind) cannot be made to depend on the restricted individuality of one man, however many people he may have about him, however racially variegated his chosen environment may be. That is all the more true inasmuch as the Roman tradition is not unique in the Church, and living historical apostolicity is not a monopoly of the Roman see, however primatial it may be.

It is pointless to emphasize and illustrate the inevitable limitations of the popes in terms of the behaviour of recent popes. For generations the faithful (and even the non-faithful) have been systematically moulded, or made to see the pope as co-extensive with the universal Church, as the instituted Church whole and entire, more than symbolically placed in the power of one man who has charge of the eternal gates of heaven or hell—and even of a little more than that in view of his supreme competence in matters of the applicability of special indulgences, and so on. The entire ecclesiastical system has been presented as deriving from a power that reached fullness through sublimation; the apotheosis of one man, as exercised by means of waterfalls and dams, canonical and hierarchical channels, controlled and officered.[8]

It was this greater degree of universalization and greater degree of restraint in the papacy that Vatican II apparently most devoutly wished in affirming on the one hand its faith in the primacy of the pope of Rome, and in proclaiming on the other hand (above all in the "indicative" vote of 30 October 1963, with an 85 per cent majority) that "episcopal collegiality" was the universal constitutional pastoral power, while including the papal function in its specifically personal aspect as something that must, consequently, be redetermined. Dogmatic development was not arrested at Vatican I or during its recurrence at Vatican II, and has not always followed a straight line.

No one could think of putting the Greek Fathers and their churches beyond the pale of authentic Christianity without doing the same for himself, or already being there himself. What do they, and what do their churches, owe to a curial and papal administration or to a still extra-collegial dogmatic papal teaching? Nothing. It is now difficult to ignore or forget that. The Church is one. The whole complex of the Roman administration, together with a specially valid canon law or universally valid religious teaching reserved to the monopoly of the pope of Rome, are not things allocated by pastoral necessity to the Petrine office. The possibility of judging their factual value after nearly two thousand years' experience is something open in the Church.

Eastern apostolic actuality does not exclude the Roman primacy, even though it does not affirm it other than as wholly subsidiary and without acknowledging in it much of what Roman

---

[8] A saint—but of his time, a very nineteenth-century saint (and very post-Vatican I) did not find any difficulty in the first commandment, "Thou shalt have none other gods but me," nor the second, "Thou shalt not take the name of the Lord thy God in vain," when he declared: "The Pope is God on earth. Jesus put the Pope above the prophets ... above the Baptis ... above the angels. Jesus put the Pope on the same level as God" (San Giovanni Bosco, *Meditazioni*, Vol. 1, Edit. 2a, pp. 80–90). That, believe it or not, was printed and disseminated in two publications, one for the use of thousands of monks and nuns, the other for the faithful, bearing the *imprimatur*, the *nihil obstat* and *cum permissu superiorum....* And there was a Holy Office not far off, a very active one, one in the pre-Vatican II style. Maximos IV expressed his indignation in a Council.

Catholics have seen or even put in it; instead the East incarnates it, implicitly, rather, in the living flux of history. More exactly, perhaps, its full Christian life, without any effectively jurisdictional Roman connections, helps it not to disembody that primacy by making Peter the only apostle, and above all by making the pope *episcopus Ecclesiae Catholicae*, the unique bishop and "form" of the universal Church.

We must remember that there is no papal sacrament, and that the life of the Church has a sacramental basis by virtue of the presence in it of the Holy Spirit, the permanent divine Vicar of Christ who is God. The collective responsibility of the episcopate (the essential consequence of the sacrament received in full collegiality) is a permanent condition. And that "qualifies" every papal act, however individual it may be. The pope is never wholly on his own. It also "qualifies" the collective or individual episcopal reactions that it might possibly evoke. St Peter admitted as much at Antioch in face of the public protests of the last of the chosen apostles, St Paul, when complaining about the universal Church and his individual responsibilities on its behalf (Gal. 2. 11–14).

Paul was chosen after the Resurrection, after Pentecost, outside the temporal life-span of Christ, within the atmosphere established by the Pentecostal event in which the apostolate of Paul is situated, distinct from those of the twelve historical witnesses. Matthais had effectively replaced Judas, and the apostolic "assembly" was reconstituted and completed with the twelve witnesses of the life of Christ and of his resurrection. We must remember, too, that beforehand the same Peter (the ineluctable model for all the popes) allowed himself to be sent collegially together with John into Samaria by the other apostles (Acts 8. 14).

Rome knows well that the Orthodox, with whom only "another step has to be taken to reach full communion" (to say nothing of the Anglicans and Protestants), will never accept the primacy as at present practised, and still less the interpretation of conciliar texts subsequent to the separation, and favouring that practice.[9]

[9] A Uniate priest who asked a sincerely ecumenistic Orthodox dignitary: "When will we get Union?" . . . "Do you know of a sane man who would put the rope round his own neck?" was the reply.

When I said to Patriarch Athenagoras in the course of a long conversation: "Neither Vatican I nor Vatican II is acceptable to Orthodoxy, we'll have to have something else," he said: "How right you are." Despite the implicit compliment, "I have to acknowledge the truth of his remark. Perhaps, in order to get this "something else", we have (more easily than in the case of the Bible and the gospels) to break down, on the hard facts, all those Catholic conciliar texts on which there is a sort of apostolic Eastern Orthodox mortgage, of churches treated as if they were apart from the "people of God", availing for this purpose of criteria ignored by their Fathers, doctors of the universal Church. They are left out of account especially by referring to that exclusively Roman axiom (shown to be non-existent in the spirit of the non-papal Fathers) which requires that in every hypothesis (and privatively in regard to any other see) that communion should exist with the see of Rome before a canonically valid situation can be said to obtain.[10]

When broken on the hard stones of history, a lot of things lose in inflexibility. There are many saints in the long line of popes. The East and West praise the Lord for that. As in all dynasties there is no dearth of average men. There are some names recurring throughout centuries—the tenth century in particular, or the sixteenth—about whom it is difficult to say whether they mean much to anyone. It is not so much a question of their personal conduct. The least said the better in that regard. Paradoxically, it is from among the company of those gentlemen that a little light is shed on our problem. I am thinking of Pope Formosus, the posthumous victim of a very close though not direct successor. The latter died a little later; he was strangled by the Roman crowd as a punishment for his crime against his predecessor's exhumed body.[11] What sort of obedience would the entire Cath-

[10] The actuality is so great that it would lose effect as evidence if cut up into "proofs". But here is quite a major example: the "schism of Antioch". For eighty-four years, the entire East, from the time of Basil, Gregory and Chrysostom, accepted an episcopal dynasty of Antioch that was rejected by Rome—the dynasty of SS. Melitus and Flavian. But that accepted by the Roman pope and—conjointly—by Egypt, was declared "schismatic", together with its supporters, formally and on several occasions, by St John Chrysostom in his popular sermons. Whenever he speaks of "schism" or of "schismatics" it is of that "schism" and those "schismatics" (cf., e.g., P.G., XII, 88, *Homily on the Epistle to the Ephesians*).

olic episcopate owe this successor of Formosus if he were again adjudged to have been pope? And if he wasn't, who would canonically decide his obvious *ipso facto* deposition if not the episcopate? Therefore the obedience of the episcopate towards the pope, however sacred it may be, is of a very special kind. It is the obedience of co-responsible individuals, co-responsible not by delegation or participation, but as of right; co-responsible individuals who might constitutionally become (at least to "certify" a situation) the pope's judges. We can go further (without referring to Constance): we at last agree openly that the wrongs of the great Christian breaks are shared; wrongs that made our divisions into separate churches inevitable. Despite the diminution brought about by those separations, all those churches were morally, existentially and spiritually entitled to, and in, their new forms.

In regard to doctrine, even if, strictly, there is no question of faith, history also moderates many things without cancelling the authoritative function of the Roman see at the centrepoint of the churches—its traditional place. The Galileo case is a classic one. This scientist was sentenced to the rack for disobeying the doctrinal authority of the Holy See. The point at issue was scientific, even though the power administering the sentence considered it to be religious. But to make such a mistake about the nature of the matter to be judged and to pronounce a religious sentence on the individual concerned is to make two rather than one doctrinal errors. Another, less widely known, though none the less classic case is the bull *Unam Sanctam* of Boniface VIII. Who today holds his teaching on the power of popes in matters temporal over the baptized and non-baptized, which is nevertheless a doctrine enjoined in a papal bull? However, the ordinary function of papal teaching is maintained, but as what in fact it is: a prime guide without any absoluteness. Apart from the rare cases of infallibility, which always require, among other conditions, the verifiable living unity of the pope with the episcopate, with the Church, and not only the unity of the Church, of the episcopate, as subordinated to the pope.[12] Hence in those papal

---

[11] See Louis Duchesne, *Les Premiers Temps de l'Etat Pontifical*; mainly chapters 15 to 19, and especially pp. 301–4.

[12] Here again we raise the question of the validity of Roman Catholic

definitions which are termed infallible, the pope does not impose his faith on the Church and does not act alone in "projecting" it into the Church, but by an act of his office authenticates a living, lived and verifiable element of the faith of the Church. Papal declarations, because of the inadequacy of human language, can lead to reactions like those classic ones after the most sacred ecumenical councils—sometimes very long-term reactions,[13] but ones which usually end (or should end) in resolving themselves in formulations which are richer because true, and more beneficial as principles of action.

V. After the Council

"It's a tragedy!" exclaimed an American seminarist one morning in the murk of a St Peter's still awaiting the bishops. He was passing a few feet away from me towards the end of the third session, the day after the most tense occasion of Vatican II—when most of the Fathers had greeted with tumultuous applause the end of Bishop de Smet's (Bruges) address. In fact the tragedy which the Catholic Church is experiencing openly or—more seriously perhaps—in silence, began that day in a public blow which was the final avowal of something more than a long reciprocal irritation between Parliament and the Throne. Parliament left as if dissolved, canonically extinct. Having dispersed, the conciliar Fathers returned to their churches: the Christian people and their priests who, after four years of elevated conciliar debates, were following the process throughout the world, were looking for renewal. The Throne remained. It remained solitary, without any complementary counterpart, without any qualified representation, on the spot, of the episcopate enjoying collegial

---

conciliar definitions, especially those concerning the papacy, arrived at without the presence or free agreement of the episcopate and the apostolic Orthodox churches of the East. The difficulty from the Roman side would be not so much the putting forward sincerely of a solution that might be thought to be valid, as—simultaneously—to believe that it was acceptable to those who (considering the tradition of the apostolic churches as a whole) had not previously chosen Rome in preference ... right up to eventual "collegial" developments.

[13] For instance there is the non-monophysitism of the non-Chalcedonian churches. This is something more generally accepted today after 1500 years of widespread contrary statements.

authority together with the Holy Father—as very large numbers of people, conciliar and extra-conciliar, had certainly hoped.

The "bishops' synod", an attempt to correct this imbalance of a dispersed Council and a Curia in place (as relieved at the Council's dispersal as it had been anxious at its convocation and ungracious about its course), is perhaps less of an answer to this state of things than even certain actions of Pope Paul. Contrary to the expectations of several Fathers and of a very large Catholic and non-Catholic public, the synod, as constituted, is hardly legally, and to date hardly in fact, anything more than an assembly of expert advisers. Each of the two meetings after the first was preceded by curial decisions settling, some weeks before the arrival of the synodal Fathers in Rome, problems on which, it seemed, they had been asked to take the trouble to pronounce together.

The internal ecclesial problems of present-day Catholicism and the ecumenical problem appear as one and the same question: Is the Christian Church, that of Jesus of Nazareth, only Roman and ultimately dictatorial and imperial—a religious sublimation of Augustus? Is there some ecclesial personality who is in communion with the Roman Throne who can stand up like a credible authority and not as a radically subordinate one—that of the loyal functionary—before the mortal person of the pope, or even face to face with some of his principal aides?

There is the beginning of a ("indirect", considering the imperfect state of communion between Rome and Orthodoxy) reply to the abnormal complexity of the problem in Pope Paul's conduct at the papal-patriarchal meeting in Jerusalem and even more in his visit to Constantinople–Istanbul, and in the "equal terms" reception given to Patriarch Athenagoras in St Peter's. In this way, in the respect shown to the occupant of the first see in Christendom after and with that of Rome (the two Romes composing but one Rome, as Patriarch John wrote to Pope Hormisdas), the distinct individuality of all the dioceses of West and East was accorded recognition and respect. The local diocese of Rome cannot substitute itself for the "sister churches" (as the pope called them in the visit to Phanar) and cannot impose itself on them. But, in the form of the independence of its pastor in relation to his local church there has devolved on Rome (in the shape of its bishop) the task of presiding in concert with them over the harmonizing of all churches (including his own) in charity—the effective yardstick for all authority, and more especially Christian authority—originally as in later practice: "Peter, do you love me... ? Feed my lambs... my sheep. ..."

It is difficult, when faced with this highly symbolic evocation of the *"Episcopus Ecclesiae Catholicae"* and of the "Ecumenical Patriarch" sitting side by side as brothers and supervisors of a fundamentally single dual tradition, to suppress the memory (even though an apparent paradox) of Pope Gregory rejecting these two titles,[14] obviously fearing that they were being given a strained and false interpretation, and not that held differently in Rome and in Constantinople. ...

I cite finally a few lines from the same St Gregory, the Pope of Rome, writing to the Pope of Alexandria, the Melkite Eulogos: "You address me with the words, 'as you have ordered'. This word 'ordered' I must ask you to withdraw as far as I am concerned, for I know who I am and who you are. You are my brother in dignity and my father in virtue.... Unfortunately, in the preamble of your letter you use that proud title 'universal Pope'. I ask you not to do so again. For what is attributed to another to a degree greater than reason demands diminishes you. And I do not look upon as an honour any honour by which my brothers lose their own honour. For my honour is the honour of the Universal Church, and the power of my brothers upheld. Therefore I am truly honoured when the honour due to my brothers is not denied them, each in his degree."[15]

Translated by V. Green

[14] *"Papa universalis"* as rejected by St Gregory is less strong than *"Episcopus Ecclesiae Catholicae"* assumed by Pius XI in a universalizing transformation of its early sense of "local", diocesan, in face of the "Novationist" bishop of Rome. The expression was solemnized by Paul VI as governing all the Acts of Vatican II.

[16] Migne P.L., LXXVII, 952. In *Pastor Aeternus* (cap. III, par. 3), Vatican I cites the two last sentences of this text while omitting the preceding one, which reads thus: "Non honorem meum esse deputo, in quo fratres meos honorem suum perdere cognosco." This omission occurred in spite of a sincere request from the (minority) conciliar Fathers for the insertion of these words in order to avoid making St Gregory say something else in his letter, or even the contrary of what he actually says. "Ut facilius sensus intelligatur" say our bishops, with the gentle irony of those who have lost before the game begins.

Ronald Modras

The Elimination of Pluralism between Churches through Pluralism within Churches

NOT ONLY within Roman Catholicism but within other Christian traditions as well, pluralism has become both undeniable and deserving of serious theological reflection. The phenomenon is hardly a new one. Orthodox churches traditionally have demonstrated divergence along national lines. Anglican and Protestant churches have long been denominated as high or low in their liturgy, fundamentalist or critical in their interpretation of Scripture, evangelical or Social Gospel oriented in their sense of mission. No matter how much a monolith it may have seemed to become in the era of the Counter-Reformation, Roman Catholicism did at least espouse the ideal of being Catholic as well as Roman and bore with it the tradition of being a *complexio oppositorum*.

Divergence in doctrine and disagreement on organizational form and ritual have resulted in the past in a splintering of Christianity into diverse churches, traditions, denominations and sects. What sociologists of religion perceived ten years ago in America, however, is becoming increasingly apparent elsewhere. While, in some respects, a homogenization of theological viewpoints is making traditional denominationalism an anachronism, new divergences are emerging within Christianity. Differences, sometimes both vast and profound, are arising within the same churches, serving to align various groups more closely to certain of their "separated brethren" than to most of their own co-religionists.[1]

[1] C. Glock and R. Stark, *Religion and Society in Tension* (Chicago, 1965), p. 117.

A literal interpretation of the Virgin Birth and belief in the existence of a personal devil aligns curial cardinals more closely to Southern Baptists than to Roman Catholics in America.[2] Whether basing themselves on the verbal inspiration of the Scriptures or the infallibility of conciliar statements, Protestant and Catholic inquisitors dedicated to maintaining doctrinal orthodoxy have more in common with each other than with their fellow churchmen who approach both Scripture and Tradition with critical historical hermeneutics. Pentecostal Christians, whether Catholic, Protestant or Orthodox, often feel more comfortable with each other than with the members of their own churches who have not shared in their own particularly intense form of religious experience. No matter what religious tradition they come from, adherents of the Social Gospel, meeting at a demonstration for peace, political liberation or social justice, find bonds of kinship with one another that they do not share with their less activist fellow church members back home.

While contrasts still divide Catholic and Protestant churches, they often seem inconsequential in comparison to the differences found within these churches themselves. "New and relatively unmarked cleavages have emerged within the Christian community that may well hold a greater potential for factionalism than did older disputes."[3] Is factionalism the inevitable upshot of innerchurch pluralism? A cursory and necessarily schematic glance at the early church may provide some clue towards an answer.

I. THE NEW TESTAMENT CHURCH

With all the concern it demonstrates for unity, the New Testament gives ample evidence for anything but accord in the first-century church.[4] In the earliest Christian community in Jerusalem, the "murmuring of the Hellenists against the Hebrews" (Acts 6. 1) resulted not only from linguistic differences but from a radically different conception of the force of the Mosaic law. The Jews could not tolerate the freedom with respect to the law exercised by Stephen and the Hellenists (Acts 6. 14), yet at the

[2] Ibid., pp. 95, 98.   [3] Ibid., p. 117.
[4] E. Käsemann, Essays on New Testament Themes (London, 1964), pp. 95-107.

same time they permitted James the brother of the Lord and his followers to remain in Jerusalem right up to the year 60. From its outset there was an obvious division in the Jerusalem church. "At the moment of persecution the primitive community embodied two groups which were already so clearly distinct even to outsiders that the one was persecuted, the other left unharmed."[5]

The question of the abiding force of the law continued to divide the early church into distinct camps, represented by James on the right, Paul on the left, and Peter vacillating between the two (Gal. 2). Nothing indicates quite so pointedly, though, the differences in the New Testament church as the existence at Corinth of Christians who would proclaim allegiance to the heavenly Christ and at the same time could curse the earthly Jesus with an "anathema" (1 Cor. 12. 3).[6] The name of Christ held together Judaizers on one side of the spectrum and pneumatic enthusiasts on the other, those who regarded the past with its traditions as absolute and others who rejected it altogether.

Even apart from these excesses, the theology of Paul is not that of John, and tensions, if not outright contradictions, can be perceived between Paul and James on the nature of faith (Gal. 2. 16; Jas. 2. 19) and between Paul and Luke on what constitutes apostleship (Gal. 1. 15 ff.; Acts 1. 21 f.). As with doctrine, so too with ministerial structure, the New Testament evinces the widest diversity: presbyteral structures in Jewish Christian communities such as Jerusalem; charismatic structures in Gentile churches such as Corinth. "Pluriform structure is general in the New Testament. Nothing suggests a uniform structure imposed from above."[7] If one adds to this the plurality of liturgical formulas, represented by differences in the Lord's Prayer (Mt. 6. 9 ff.; Lk. 11. 2 ff.) and the formulas of institution in the Last Supper accounts (Mk. 14. 22 ff.; Lk. 22. 15 ff.; 1 Cor. 11. 23 ff.); the differences between the Synoptics and John in their accounts of Jesus' preaching and ministry; the very fact of four gospels instead of one, a fact which was to cause some difficulty to the Church in the next century (as indicated by the harmonization

[5] E. Haenchen, *The Acts of the Apostles* (Philadelphia, 1971), p. 266.

[6] Cf. W. Schmithals, *Gnosticism in Corinth* (New York, 1971).

[7] J. McKenzie, "Ministerial Structures in the New Testament", *Concilium*, April 1972 (American Edn., vol. 74), p. 22.

attempted by Tatian in his *Diatessaron*), it becomes clear that, although bound together by faith in one God, one Lord and one baptism, the church of the New Testament evinced extremes of diversity which seem to us today almost inconceivable.

While recognizing within the New Testament a unity of faith, one must also admit to the presence there of distinct differences in perspective, emphasis and approach. The New Testament reflects a plurality of writers with different theologies, drawing from divergent traditions, speaking to a variety of missionary situations. A critical historical approach to the Bible does not permit levelling down all these differences to a common denominator or indiscriminately harmonizing the tensions among them. On the contrary, taking the New Testament seriously as a norm for theology (Constitution on Revelation, 21) means taking the New Testament as a whole, its concern for unity along with its rejection of uniformity. The establishment of a *regula fidei*, the canon of the New Testament and the monarchial episcopate were measures necessary to ensure the unity of the Church in the second century, but even then unity did not mean uniformity and did not obviate the possibility of conflicts between Irenaeus and Pope Victor, Cyprian and Pope Stephen, Alexandria and Antioch and East and West.

For one who would idealize the Church and disregard its thoroughly human dimension by concentrating exclusively on its theological character, the existence of divergent theologies, pluriform structures, and consequent conflicts, power struggles, and partisanship in the earliest church may come as something of an embarrassment. Such idealization, however, is tantamount to an ecclesial form of monophysitism. To the student of the social sciences, the Church is a social entity, subject to the laws and dynamics of all social entities. Grace does not destroy nature, and, whether considered a community of faith, the people of God or the Body of Christ, the Church is none the less a community, a group of people, a social body. As such, the Church is susceptible to the ambiguities of all social bodies—to social stratification; to the rise and fall of élites; to conflict between freedom and organization; and, by all means, to factionalization into parties, sub-groups, right and left wing, proponents of the *status quo* and innovators, controlling factions and opposing forces.

Like any social body, the Church can learn from the findings of the social sciences, particularly with regard to the question of pluralism.

II. THE SOCIOLOGY OF PLURALISM

Although variously assessed, group pluralism is a general characteristic of all human society. The social sciences today recognize the plurality of group structures as an assured datum of every form of human existence, whether in a complex society or in intermediary groups.[8] From the time of Hobbes and Rousseau, the plurality of groups has been met by some with apprehension, regarded not only as a loss of unity but also a source of anarchy. Sociological data, however, permit us today to see plurality of groups as providing a potential for freedom and a means of diminishing suppression and coercion. No group, any more than any one man, can provide all the answers to a question, all the solutions to a problem.

The contention that plurality necessarily destroys unity is an unfounded and unreflected postulate. A certain amount of nonconformity is endemic or chronic, in fact, intrinsic in the operation of all communities.[9] Institutionalized conflict, exemplified by parliamentary debate, the American system of checks and balances in government, or the British concept of the "loyal opposition", may be regarded as an organizing rather than a disjunctive factor, a *sine qua non* for assuring stability in a society and for preventing too great a concentration of power in any one person or group. Even the conflict which derives from pluralism is an important element of social interaction. Far from being a negative factor that always rends communities apart, social conflict may contribute to the maintenance of community, in that conflict and co-operation are not separable states but rather distinct phases of one and the same process. A society without conflicts, in which nothing needs to be changed, in which all functions are maintained in perfect equilibrium, constitutes a utopian

[8] A. Gehring, "Zur Theorie der pluralistischen Gesellschaft", *Stimmen der Zeit* 189 (1972), pp. 237–47.
[9] J. Bernard, "Community Disorganization", *International Encyclopedia of the Social Sciences* (New York, 1968), III, pp. 163–8.

fantasy; to attempt to realize such a society could have only totalitarian consequences. "Even the thought of a society without conflict is an act of violence against human nature."[10]

If a community is to survive, however, together with the plurality of groups within it, there must be conjoined a guarantee of unity, a common bond that embraces all parties, an encompassing consensus that supersedes all else. This all-embracing consensus provides a foundation acceptable to all the members in a community together with a source of common identity. Community of any kind implies some minimum of consensus, although in no society is consensus ever shared with equal intensity or concern.[11] Consensual unity depends on loyalty, a sense of attachment to someone, some thing, some cause. For Christians the object of that loyalty is the person and cause of Jesus Christ. He is the foundation of the Church, the object of its faith, and the source of identity which permits the Church the widest of diversity, even with respect to doctrine.

III. DOCTRINAL DIVERSITY

The Church is a communal response to the revelation of God in Jesus Christ. Christian revelation is not a compilation of revealed truths but a person (Constitution on Revelation, 6). For this reason, and in virtue of the original unity and totality of revelation in him, Jesus has been called the "primordial dogma" of Christianity.[12] Christian faith finds in Jesus the one word through whom God has expressed his innermost being. Expressing that faith to others requires human conceptualization and reflection. This has necessarily led to a plurality of doctrinal formulas, a plurality whose diversity has become as problematic as it is human.

One of the most consequential teachings of Vatican II was the affirmation of legitimate diversity in theology (Decree on Ecumenism, 4). So too was the Council's attitude towards differ-

[10] R. Dahrendorf, *Gesellschaft und Freiheit* (Munich, 1968), p. 128, cited in A. Gehring, *op. cit.*
[11] E. Schils, "The Concept of Consensus", *International Encyclopedia of the Social Sciences* (New York, 1968), III, p. 262.
[12] W. Seibel, "Der eine Glaube und die Vielfalt der Dogmen", *Stimmen der Zeit*, 169 (1961–62), pp. 264–77.

ences in doctrinal expression between the Orthodox East and Roman Catholic West, the admission that these differences are "often to be considered as complementary rather than conflicting" (Decree on Ecumenism, 17). The *depositum fidei*, which found its first crystallization in the New Testament consists not only of the revelation of God in Jesus but also of the human comprehension and expression of that revelation. The mystery revealed in Jesus as the Christ was such as to require a variety of symbols, images and theologies to express its plenitude in the first-century Church. For the same reason, a diversity of doctrinal expression is still required.

Vatican II affirmed the legitimacy of diversity in theology and tradition among differing cultures and ethnic groups. Similarly, there is no reason why a diversity in dogma cannot be affirmed as well.[13] Dogmatic statements may not be elevated above the realm of the human, historically conditioned and relative, as if they were not themselves the canonized expression of a particular theology at a particular point in space and time. As Karl Rahner has pointed out, dogma results from a communal experience of a divine reality, an experience conditioned and stamped by the thought and language of the community which experienced it.[14]

If the concept of dogmatic diversity seems to pose a threat to the unity of Christian faith, it might be remembered that, as conceived by the early church, a dogma is a liturgical statement, and liturgy itself has doctrinal implications (*lex orandi, lex credendi*). Diversity of dogma need not prejudice the unity of faith any more than diversity of worship and liturgical practice. Precisely such variety of doctrinal and ritual expression is required in order to reflect the plenitude of Christian revelation. Although one may be more adequate than another, no historical tradition can say all that is to be said about God, man and the revelation of God in Christ. It should be expected, therefore, that both doctrinal and ritual expression of Christian faith be as rich and diverse as human language and culture, as men's experience of God and the New Testament church's experience of Christ,

---

[13] Cf. G. Dejaifve, "Diversité dogmatique et unité de la Révélation", *Nouvelle Revue Théologique*, 89 (1967), pp. 16–25.

[14] K. Rahner, *Theological Investigations* (Baltimore, 1966), V, pp. 42–66.

for these all have served as important sources of pluralism in the Church.

IV. Sources of Pluralism

From its very beginning both *language and culture* have served as sources of pluralism in the Church (Acts 6). Diversity of language is an expression of the diversity of the human experience of God and his creation. Differences among languages are such that an exact translation of the gospel from one language to another is impossible without something being lost and something else acquired. Witness the differences between Hebrew and Greek in such concepts as truth, spirit and justice. In leaving its original Jewish milieu and going out to the Gentiles, the Church necessarily underwent enrichment and change, as it accommodated itself to new missionary situations and became "all things to all men".

Likewise the *philosophical and cultural categories* through which Christian revelation has been expressed have each contributed to pluralism in the Church. Early Christian writers drew freely from the Stoicism and Neo-Platonism of their day, just as Aquinas drew from Aristotle, and today's theologians draw from existentialism. Each new casting of the Christian message has effected new and distinct differences in the Church, its teaching and self-expression.

Another source of pluralism is the *dialectical nature of religious experience*. Influenced by Rudolf Otto's *The Idea of the Holy* and the twofold aspect of the experience of the sacred as a *mysterium tremendum et fascinosum*, Paul Tillich distinguished between the priestly and prophetic elements in all religion.[15] Both elements are in every personal experience of God as well as in every communitarian expression of faith. Because man is finite, however, he can never maintain both aspects in perfect balance. One element will invariably outweigh the other.

In churches such as the Catholic and Orthodox where the priestly element holds sway, the holy is experienced primarily as a *mysterium fascinosum*, as present here and now, grasping us through the medium of a person, event or thing. Such churches

---

[15] P. Tillich, *Dynamics of Faith* (London, 1957), pp. 56–69.

have a distinct sacramental and incarnational orientation. Persons, objects and actions are seen as enjoying a consecration independent of their individual character or moral worth. Because holiness is viewed as a present reality and not a moral demand, one is born into such churches and his sins do not negate membership. Such churches look to the past and to tradition, emphasizing the already present aspect of realized eschatology. They are in constant danger of falling into the idolatry of absolutizing their sacred books, doctrines, rituals and symbols, in that these bearers of the holy are identified with the holy itself.

In several churches in the Protestant tradition where the prophetic element holds sway, the holy is experienced primarily as a *mysterium tremendum*, as a demand for moral perfection. Such churches place a high premium on adherence to a revealed law, which is viewed as both a gift and a command of God. Membership in such churches depends on a free decision and a certain degree of moral perfection, so that they tend to become theocratic, striving to bring personal morals and social institutions into conformity with the law of God. In churches of this stamp, preaching of the word is emphasized together with the "not yet" of futuristic eschatology. The danger confronting such churches is that of becoming intellectualistic and moralistic, of losing a sense of the sacramental experience of God and thereby becoming thoroughly secular.

A further sources of pluralism among churches is the *tendency in all of them to concentrate upon one part of the New Testament* to the exclusion of others. It was the heresy of Marcionism to attempt to simplify Christianity by reducing it to Paulinism. A similar temptation has plagued Protestantism for much of its history with a resultant multiplicity of denominations and sects. Protestant churches no longer omit certain books from the canon, as Marcion did, but many still tend to focus on certain books of the New Testament to all but the complete exclusion of others. Lutherans concentrate upon Paul, especially his epistles to the Galatians and Romans. Pentecostal, Spirit-centred churches favour the Acts of the Apostles, especially chapter 2, and 1 Corinthians, chapters 12 and 14. Liberal Christians and proponents of the Social Gospel concentrate on the Synoptics, especially the Sermon on the Mount.

Selectivity of concentration has not, however, been a failing restricted to Protestant churches. Certainly John "the theologian" has had a greater impact on the Orthodox churches than Paul. Matthew 16. 18 and the "early Catholicism" of the pastoral epistles have been far more central to Roman Catholicism than Paul's teaching on charism or justification. The christology of the Prologue to John's gospel has been more developed in both Catholic and Orthodox churches than the christology of the Synoptics.

V. Conclusions

In the face of the pluralism and divergence within so many churches today, what can be done to prevent further fragmentation? In the face of the pluralism and divergence dividing churches, what can be done to heal the schisms to which differences, doctrinal and otherwise, have given rise? In the light of the foregoing, we are now prepared to draw several conclusions:

1. *Pluralism*, whether of doctrine, liturgical practice or ecclesial structures, *should not be seen as necessarily destructive or dangerous* to the unity and well-being of the Church. To quote Pope Paul VI: "In the ecclesial field, too, the complexity of its doctrinal, hierarchical, ritual and moral components cannot be expressed in any other way than through pluralistic words and pluralistic forms. ... We are pluralists precisely because we are Catholics, which means universal."[16] The very catholicity of the Church demands pluralism. The tension and conflict which inevitably accrue to diversity need not be detrimental but rather creative and constructive.

2. The legitimacy of pluralism within the Church *is not without limits*, however. There is a point at which plurality becomes promiscuity, at which the desire for enrichment becomes simply the excuse to introduce foreign elements into Christian faith and practice. To counteract precisely the attempt by Gnosticism to introduce such incompatible foreign elements into Christianity, the Church established the canon of the Scriptures. In so doing,

[16] *The Pope Speaks*, 14 (1969), p. 117 ("Abbiamo altre volte parlato", *L'Osservatore Romano*, 15 May 1969).

it rejected any number of claims made for secret apostolic traditions and recognized the books of the New Testament as the ultimate norm which judges any doctrine or practice and determines whether or not it deserves the name Christian. (Cf. Vatican II, Const. on Divine Rev., 10, 24.) The Church is not a law unto itself. Its tradition and magisterium stand in submission to the person and teaching of Jesus. Comprising with their plurality of forms and formulas a witness to the revelation first recorded in the New Testament, both post-biblical tradition and the magisterium serve as secondary sources and guides. Their testimony is derived from and therefore subordinate to Scripture, alone the Church's *norma normans non normata*.

3. Within the framework of the New Testament, *a broad latitude is permitted for pluralism of doctrine, practice and ecclesial structure*. If Christianity has developed into a *complexio oppositorum*, it is because the New Testament itself is a *complexio oppositorum*. In order to be true to their New Testament origins, it is necessary for all Christians to take the entire New Testament seriously, avoiding the kind of *hairesis* which take a book and makes it the entire Bible, which selects a part of the canon and elevates it to a "canon within the canon". Obviously not all the witnesses of the New Testament are to be put on the same level. Not all the writings have the same value. It is necessary to differentiate between primary and secondary witnesses in the New Testament on the basis of chronology, authenticity and that which is distinctively Christian.

On the other hand, legitimate emphases on certain parts of the New Testament should not be permitted to become principles of exclusion. Protestants have often been guilty of the sin of Marcion, attempting to reduce Christianity to Paulinism, to a "pure gospel". Catholics have sinned in the direction of the Gnostics, opening Christianity up to extra-evangelical elements in the name of unwritten tradition or dogmatic development. Both extremes stand in contradiction to the early Church, in which catholic pluralism was combined with "evangelical concentration" (H. Küng). If the entire New Testament is seen as validly claiming to be the Church's ultimate norm, then Protestants must take the "early Catholicism" of the New Testament seriously and

Catholics must recognize Matthew 16. 18 and the Pastoral epistles within the broader, more distinctively Christian framework of charism. It has been said that "over-emphasis upon one favourite point is an occupational disease of theology".[17] Be that as it may, a hazard for theology should not become institutionalized into a church, and certainly not into a church formally divided from other churches. Fidelity to the New Testament requires that all Christian communities strive to witness to the diversity expressed there.

4. The variety of doctrinal statements, theologies and ecclesial structures evidenced in the New Testament *does not permit any church to raise exclusive or absolute claims for its particular teachings or practice.* There is no dogma, ritual or organizational structure that stands above history and, therefore, the possibility of needing reform. There is no theology, whether that of Augustine, Aquinas, Luther or Calvin, that cannot be corrected, improved or surpassed. There is no church structure, whether papal, episcopal, presbyteral or congregational, that can claim exclusive apostolic origins. Church order today can and should remain open in principle to all the possibilities which existed in the New Testament church. Factionalism and schism cannot help but result when that which is human is considered divine, when that which is accidental is considered essential, when that which is peripheral is considered central, when that which is conditioned by history is considered irreformable and absolute.

5. Formidable as was plurality and diversity both within and between the churches of the New Testament, *the differences were not such as to disrupt unity.* They were not such as to prevent intercommunion between Jerusalem and Corinth, Antioch and Rome. One faith, one Lord, one baptism did not exclude the possibility of differences, disagreement and even conflict, but the premium placed upon charity succeeded in preventing a break. Schisms have traditionally been seen with good reason as sins against charity. It was not the existence of differences that Paul criticized in Corinth (1 Cor. 1), but the contentions, envy, strife, the boasting and self-glorification. Such attitudes contradict Paul's subsequent description of love as patient, kind, not jealous,

[17] J. Pelikan, *Obedient Rebels* (New York, 1964), p. 203.

not insisting on its own way, but bearing all things, enduring all things (1 Cor. 13). Charity requires of groups, no less than of individuals, a toleration of differences, a willingness to live with the creative tensions that result from them, and the patience of Gamaliel to wait and see if an innovation is the work of God or not.

No less than any other community, a church characterized by pluralism, if it is to survive, must be founded upon a consensus, a common bond, a sense of loyalty that surpasses all other differences. Churches distinguished from one another by divergence can overcome their divisions only in terms of such a superseding loyalty. For Christians, the object of their loyalty, their ultimate source of unity, cannot be a doctrine, a set of rituals, or a system of organization. *The fundamental source of unity* for the Church today, the ultimate object of its loyalty, *can be only the person and cause of Jesus and the conviction that he is Christ and Lord.* This loyalty and conviction, which united the many divergent churches of the first century, permitted the diverse witnesses of the New Testament to be joined into one canon. This same loyalty and conviction can serve to overcome the divisions between churches today and permit them to look at one another and their traditions with a sense of mutual belonging. Then, to paraphrase Terence, Christians will be able to look at one another's differences and say: *Christianus sum; Christiani nihil a me alienum puto.*

Should there be Parties in the Church in the Future?

(a) *An Orthodox Answer*

Nikos Nissiotis

I. Different Types

IN THIS article, the word "party" is used in the wider sense of "group" and it is, of course, well known that there have always been groups in the Church working, in a more or less open opposition to authority and the institutional Church, for renewal. In most cases, these groups have consisted of priests and laymen sharing the same ideas and inspired by the same prophetic impulse whose aim has been to correct and renew the life of the Church. There have, however, been different types of renewal movements, following different paths and using different methods. The results that they have achieved have also been different, in accordance with their understanding of the term "in the Church" and the way in which they have put this concept into practice. Both in theory and in practice, they have always been subject to the influence of ecclesiological and confessional presuppositions, historical circumstances and local conditions.

Some of these groups, then, have remained literally "in the Church", others have remained in it, but rather as a "state" within the "State", with their own inner discipline, and others have left the Church, set up other churches and asserted their complete independence of the authority of the Church that has rejected them. Groups of this third type have always disputed the value of the authority and institutional nature of the Church as an established historical structure and have insisted that authority stems from the qualities of those able to work for the renewal of the Church.

By parties or groups "in the Church", however, we mean above all those movements of liturgical, evangelical or moral renewal within the Church which tend to express themselves as associations of Christians who are independent of hierarchical authority even if they are led by priests. The aim of such groups has almost always been to revitalize ordinary members of the Church in neglected aspects of the life of the Church.

Movements of this type are known in all the churches and generally speaking their influence is good. In Greece and the Lebanon as well as in the West, they have been responsible for biblical, missionary, liturgical and catechetical renewal in the Church. Sometimes, of course, they have tended to be exclusive, scornful of the Church's authority or even puritanical. In Greece today, for example, there are movements which are becoming extremely conservative and even anti-ecumenical, thus going contrary to the Orthodox Church as a whole at the present time. In the main, however, the renewal movements have made an enormous positive contribution to the life of the Eastern Church.

Sectarian movements which end by claiming to be new churches, but which are really no more than para-ecclesial groups, are, however, not possible in Eastern Christianity, above all because they give rise to the acute problem of eucharistic communion. In the Orthodox view, the Church is not simply an institution. It is above all the people of God gathered in one place around the Eucharist celebrated by the bishop or the priest who represents him in the diocese. The Church is, of course, an institution with rules pertaining to its hierarchical structure, but it is also an event, in which all believers reaffirm their deep, mystical and spiritual union in one, undivided Church at all times and in all places. So much has been written about this subject in recent years that it would be useless to discuss it in detail here. I would draw the reader's attention to the published papers of the second Cerdic conference at Strasbourg (13–15 May 1971)[1] and, among these, especially those by the Catholic theologian

---

[1] *Les groupes informels dans l'Église. Deuxième colloque du Cerdic, Strasbourg, 13–15 mai 1971* (Université des Sciences humaines de Strasbourg, 1971), p. 309; this publication contains many contributions concerned with our subject, written from the sociological, political, historical and theological points of view.

Yves Congar (pp. 273–300), the Orthodox theologian Jean
Zizioulas (pp. 251–73) and the Protestant theologian Roger Mehl
(pp. 235–51).

II. Groups of Political Contestation in the Church?

If I understand it correctly, these authors are concerned with
the special situation that has recently arisen in connection with
the emergence of groups of radical political contestation within
the different churches. These groups are opposed to the authority
of the churches, question their hierarchical structure and dispute
their close links with the establishment and their reluctance to
be politically and socially committed. They accuse the churches of
wanting to preserve the *status quo* and of refusing to adopt radical, revolutionary policies opposed to the capitalist, consumer
society. On the other hand, they make no direct attempt to find
out whether they are, from the ecclesiological point of view, sectarian. They are groups "in the Church". They reveal no typi-
cally sectarian tendencies. They do not aim to form new
churches. Their sectarianism is to be found in their attitude of
radical contestation. They remain *in* the Church in order to pose
the question of the true interpretation of the gospel as the total
commitment of the Church to political activity.

Correctly interpreted, this problem is, I believe, connected with
what these groups represent by their radical demand for political
commitment and with the value of this attitude to the whole
Church. Certainly this aspect of the problem is the most urgent
one today and more important than the ecclesiological position
occupied by these groups. At the level of ecclesiology, the Orthodox reply would probably be: "These groups must be in the
Church, but they should not become churches within the Church
and leave the mother Church to found new churches."

It is indeed very difficult to find an answer to the question
asked in the title of this article if it is really concerned with the
radical spirit of political contestation of these groups in the
Church, their radical attitude and their need to translate their
faith into political activism. To do so, it is necessary to analyse
the causes of the radical attitude of these groups and the attitude
of the churches towards their political and social commitment.

The first point to note is that this radical political commitment, this restlessness with regard to the consumer society and this reaction against the establishment is general nowadays, especially among young people. There are no longer any ethical principles, beliefs or ideologies which prepare individuals, by theory or by observation of society, for this kind of moral action. This preparation takes place in action. The best theory is the application of the theory in action. The true ideology is the ideology that has been put into practice. There is therefore a metaphysics of action and practical application which enables many people today to transcend theory—at every level, orthodoxy is judged by its orthopraxis.

There is a second aspect of this question of political commitment, namely that there can be no commitment without an unequivocal attitude towards specific political conflicts and specific problems arising from the structures of the consumer society. To remain silent in situations of this kind is to give consent to or even to collaborate with the establishment. It is also necessary to have a clear attitude towards such movements as women's liberation and racial equality.

Finally, there has to be conscious acceptance of the fact that every traditional institution is a centre of power. The institution represses new creative and revolutionary forces which are working against technocracy for the humanization of the world, against repression and violence by state bureaucracy for freedom in the world and against the exploitation of the poor nations for justice in the world. This action is absolutely and consistently logical.

This attitude, which is the driving force behind the modern revolutionary movement of young people generally, is adopted instinctively by similar groups in the Church, the members of which emphasize the revolutionary aspect of Jesus, contrasting it with the existing religious and political establishment. They insist that the whole Church should support the movements which seek to transform society and emancipate it from its existing political, social and religious structures. The Church, they believe, has the task of making itself known less as the Body of Christ in the world by means of the sacrament and more as a revolutionary movement wherever it is necessary to do this. If the Church, they claim, does not identify itself with this struggle, it can be no more than a power working to maintain the *status quo* and a repressive force. Its theology will be no more than a rational, systematic justification of this "sacred" power, the strongest means of propping up the establishment in the developed consumer society of the West.

In considering the attitude of the groups in the Church and the question that it raises, we should not lose sight of the weakness that characterizes the life of the Church, both the hierarchy and the mass of believers, in the great national churches of the so-called Christian countries. There is a noticeable apathy on the part of the established churches with regard to social and political problems which cannot be explained or excused on the basis of a principle of faith. On the other hand, however, the answer to our question does not depend so much on the Church to which we belong as on our political situation, our economic circumstances and our social structure. In my view, there can be no Orthodox answer—this would only be possible in an ecclesiological context. It would, however, be wrong to try to give an answer based exclusively on our political or social situation, since politics should not directly affect our answer. I do not think that the Christian may impose on the Church the form of politics which he regards as compatible with faith at all times and places. I agree, of course, that, in the last resort, the contestation practised by these groups in the Church is not purely political in its aims, but is rather the result of the preaching of the gospel message in a world in a state of crisis. Our answer should respect this fact.

III. The Sensitive Point

This brings us to the most sensitive point in our analysis. If these groups in the Church are really interpreting the gospel in a dynamic way, stressing the need for a revolutionary transformation of society, then this interpretation ought to have an ecclesial character. My reservations therefore apply not to the fact that this revolutionary movement exists in the Church, but rather to the conditions which lead these groups to identify themselves with a particular political movement based on a particular political ideology. I have the impression, in other words, that these groups in the Church often lose their ecclesial, evangelical and sacramental character, sacrificing it to a political identity. Shaken in their foundation in the Church, these groups clearly reverse their order of priority. "I believe, therefore I act at the political level" is often reversed, becoming "I act at the political level, therefore I believe". This is, I think, a sectarian position, since, even if these groups remain in the Church, they automatically create a sect, their new dogmatic conviction threatening to cause a schism in eucharistic communion and the communion of the word that is preached.

It is very difficult to accept the crisis of identity and the reversal in the order of priority that are caused by some of these groups in the Church, which ultimately tend to favour unilateral and extra-ecclesiastical principles as criteria for membership of the Body of Christ. This has almost always happened in the case of schismatic groups. Revolutionary or even purely political ethics can, after all, never be the only criteria for authentic membership of the Church or for a dynamic, living faith. The Church can never consist exclusively of members engaged in political contestation. To take an extreme example, membership of the Marxist movement can never be the condition for admission to a renewal group in the Church.

Clearly, the answer that we give will depend to a great extent on the degree to which these groups make the Christian message political. If, for example, a group, in what it says and does, makes that message completely political, transforming it into a Marxist or a capitalist, a communist or a fascist ideology, there is a grave danger that the group in question will no longer be in communion with and in the Church. There is also a danger that it will favour special, extra-ecclesiastical criteria for membership of the Church based on political, social or economic principles and the activism that results from these. In that case, we would have to give a negative answer to our question. After all, God is not the first politician, Christ is not the first revolutionary and the Holy Spirit is not the first to inspire revolution. The Lord's Supper is not a political action. Slogans of this kind—expressed positively, statements like this about the Trinity, and so on, are quite common these days—are unable to renew the Church. On the contrary, they tend to create a problem of identity in the Church and to weaken it when it does commit itself to political action.

Whenever they decide to act in the name of Christ the revolutionary members of these groups in the Church should ask themselves a number of questions. What is, for example, the specific task of the committed Christian? What distinguishes the Church from ideologies and above all from political parties? What is the charismatic character of the communion of the Church as an undivided Body in the political struggle for the dignity of man, justice and freedom? If the members of these groups do not ask these and similar questions within the eucharistic communion of the Church, they are bound to throw doubt on their reason for remaining in the Church.

It is not easy to characterize political or ethical activism in general. In the life of the Church, not everything is action and therefore moral, just as not everything is not faith and therefore without action. The two spheres of faith and action have to remain permanently linked, but must not be confused or without unilateral application. Activism in faith, like functionalism in philosophy and technocracy in civilization, only represent part of the truth. Before it becomes an ethical imperative, faith is an affirmation of the existence of God among us, in the coming together of his Church. Faith includes joy, hope, mystical experience, meditation and contemplation as well as political and social activism. It also includes the mysterious action of the Holy Spirit, uniting us in one Body and thus transcending our political, class and ideological differences. The same Spirit helps us to "scrutinize the signs of the times" as a community and to prepare ourselves for activity in the service of our fellow men. As members of the Church, our activity should be distinctively Christian and ecclesial and we should constantly bear in mind the motivation of a social revolution and its aims. The Church does not engage in politics, but we, as members of the Church, must undertake a continuous Christian analysis of politics and distinguish the absolute character of political action from its ideological basis. The Church may join any political movement in order to serve the dignity of man, justice and freedom, but Christians must at the same time make distinctions, if necessary place a distance between themselves and their political alliance, ask questions and act as prophets.

IV. Conclusion

We may conclude by saying that a positive answer must, after all, be given to the question asked in the title of this article.— Yes, there must be parties in the Church, renewal groups carrying out, collectively, a prophetic task. There must also be groups of the kind that we have mentioned, groups engaged in contestation, shaking the mass of Christians out of their apathy and urging them to accept their responsibilities in the world, reacting against the inertia of the Church authorities and making the members of the hierarchy conscious of the fact that external appearance, prestige and the established order are not enough. There has never in the history of the Church been such an urgent need as there is today for the immovable and often inflexible structures of the Church to be severely shaken and for Christians generally to be made less passive.

At this level, there is so much for these parties or groups to do, but they must do it *in the Church* in the fullest sense of the term and not in any way which tends towards an individualistic, sectarian or anthropocentric extremism which takes its norms from an absolutist political ideology. We must look forward to the emergence of groups of this kind throughout the Church, groups whose members know how to combine contestation with loyalty and spiritual discipline. They must, in other words, seek unity with, not separation from, the communion of faith in their contestation of the authority of the institutional Church when this reveals a neglect of the essential Christian tasks and in their opposition to the self-satisfied, middle-class attitudes of Christians living in a consumer society. If they remain conscious of the constant need for loyalty and discipline, their spirit of contestation will be a true and meaningful reflection of the life of the church community.

If all these conditions are borne in mind, these parties in the Church will be really effective, their faithfulness to the Church giving support to their efforts to make the world a more just and human place. Distinct from other action groups because of their faith and membership of the Church and distinguished by their

Christian view of mankind, these parties in the Church can play a vital part in the life of the Church and the world. Today as in the past, this task is to work for an increasingly dynamic presence of the Church in the world.

Translated by David Smith

(b) *A Protestant Answer*

Kristen Ejner Skydsgaard

THIS is not an easy question. It cannot be answered with a quick Yes or No. First of all we have to look at the problem of Church unity.

1. *True and false unity*

Applied to the Church, unity means first of all unity in the gospel, in the good news of the kingdom of God in Jesus Christ through the Holy Spirit. That is how Paul understood it in Gal. 1. 6 ff. The power which creates unity is not even a uniform creed, important though that may be; still less is it an authority with absolute power over the organization of the Church; it is the resplendent centre of the Christian faith: Jesus Christ, Kyrios, the events of his life and his preaching, his death on the cross, his resurrection and exaltation, as recorded in the New Testament and authoritatively proclaimed and taught in the Church through the Holy Spirit.

He alone is the ultimate source of the unity of the people of God in the new covenant. "He is our peace, who has made us both one, and has broken down the dividing wall of hostility, by abolishing in his flesh the law of commandments and ordinances, that he might create in himself one new man in place of the two, so making peace, and might reconcile us both to God in one body through the cross...through him we both have access in one Spirit to the Father" (Eph. 2. 14–16, 18).

The *ekklesia* of Jesus Christ is the people of God in which this gospel is present with power in word and sacrament, the community in which Jesus rules as Lord, reconciler and redeemer. It is the place where the power of love and truth which overcomes all divisions and all hostilities takes effect. That is why parties can find no place in this community; in this fellowship all estrangement, hostility and sharp opposition are impossible. Unity is not one quality which the community of Jesus possesses along with others; the community of Jesus is in itself the overcoming of hostility between different parties, classes and nations.

The community of Jesus is the guardian of this fellowship which overcomes all hostility. Its responsibility extends from the relations between two human beings to the ultimate cosmic dimension. It is not a forced unity, a unity of immobility or inertia, but a unity of freedom, variety and spiritual richness. Certainly problems can arise about fellowship in this community of unity, but they cannot be allowed to develop into a final, definitive estrangement, because in that case the vital nerve of this fellowship would be cut. The unity of the Church is always threatened by partisan individuals who like arguments and always know best; outwardly they appear pious, but inwardly they are self-seeking.

True church unity is also endangered by false prophets of unity who have forgotten what the unity of Christ means, and maintain or construct "in the name of Christ" a false unity in which parties and all deviations from "orthodoxy" are severely forbidden and suppressed. In fact they do it in their own names. To destroy the community of Christ, Antichrist can use false party divisions and false unity. There is a diabolical spirit of faction and a diabolical spirit of false peace. In the apocalyptic visions of many great poets, Antichrist appears as the prophet of peace, of the unity which will make all men happy. The unity of Antichrist can appear in religious, even in Christian, guise. That is why it is dangerous. The Church is constantly subjected to diabolical temptations. This must be so, and must be realized in the Church. Jesus was also tempted, not once but constantly. Temptation is a fundamental condition of all human existence, including the Church. There have always been times in the Church when temptation conquered; every church must realize this and admit it. There were times when a false unity had to be broken, not for the sake of destruction, but to open the way to true unity. There can be a split which does not arise out of personal argumentativeness, but out of obedience. There can be a unity which God, in his wrath and in his grace, himself breaks.

2. *Protest for the sake of the gospel*

There ought not to be parties in the Church; it is wrong for parties to exist in the sense in which the word is used here. Nevertheless there are in the history of the Church "small" or "great" moments at which the sharpest criticism must be made and a protest expressed which destroys the mere apparent unity of the Church. Why? Because God is a God of true unity, and because there have been obedient people. This can only be expressed in this paradoxical form. Paul had to break with Peter in Antioch, not out of love of argument, but out of obedience to the gospel. Both were reconciled, and gave each other the hand of fellowship. The conflict between "Jewish Christians" and "Gentile Christians" was not merely academic.

Luther had to break with Leo X and his curia, and so with the Roman Church of the time, not out of quarrelsomeness but out of obedience. He did not want the break. "God forbid, absit, absit," he said in 1519. Accuse, scold, threaten, beg: all this he was prepared to do, but not to destroy the unity of the Church for that end. Love before all things. A readiness for love's sake to put up not only with loss of material goods, but with all the horror of sin: *"Ficta charitas est, quae non nisi commoda alterius ferre potest."* Love which will only share the good fortune of others, and not bear burdens, is only appearance.[1] Yet in the end Luther had to break with Leo X, because the gospel and with it the salvation of mankind forced him to it, and the two have still not given each other the hand of fellowship, even though the differences between them today are much less.

We may perhaps ask whether there is not something like a hierarchy of parties. There are parties which do not go to the root, which are more or less "superficial" and perhaps ultimately not theological at all, but based on "non-theological factors". There are other parties which have their origin in essentials.

[1] Cf. Paul Althaus, *Die Theologie Martin Luthers* (1962), pp. 269–70.

3. *Church and truth*

It is not enough to consider decisions made in the past. We must have the courage to look at this question in the light of our situation today, since we are supposed to have learnt something from the course of history and especially from our present experience.

The starting-point for this meditation will be Jn. 16. 12–14: "I have many things to say to you, but you cannot bear them now. When the Spirit of truth comes, he will guide you into all truth; for he will not speak on his own authority, but whatever he hears he will speak, and he will declare to you the things that are to come. He will glorify me, for he will take what is mine and declare it to you."

Jesus says that he will tell his disciples through the Spirit something that at present they cannot endure. Though the word "endure" (*bastazein*) is used here in a metaphorical sense, it retains its basic meaning of bearing a burden, one's cross, enduring something which is very difficult and demands courage. At that time the disciples were unable to endure what was to be revealed to them in the future, but the Spirit, the comforter, would tell them later what they were not yet strong enough to hear. The Spirit of truth would make them free to hear, believe, understand, speak and act in situations which were to come. The Spirit's leadership is inextricably bound up with situations in the future. The meaning is not additional truths, nor can it be a dialectical or organic development of a christology existent in germ. At least, this cannot be the main thing. The truth which they have heard, seen with their eyes and touched with their hands (1 Jn. 1. 1) is to be preserved intact in the successive new situations which as yet they know nothing about. Through these constantly new situations, which will be heavy to bear, the glory of Jesus will become ever greater for them. The way of the Spirit is not easy. God's way, even with his disciples, always goes through death to life. The saying about the grain of wheat (Jn. 12. 24) applies to the Church too. On this way there are disclosures of the truth connected with the future situations. It is as if the future is taken up into the knowledge of revelation. It is not, as has been said before, a question of additional truths in the future, but of the truth of Christ in constantly new historical

situations. In other words, history and knowledge belong together. History leads to a constantly renewed understanding of
the glory of Jesus.

What does this mean today? Today the Church is going
through one of the situations which are referred to implicitly in
our text. We know more about these situations than the disciples
could then because we have a long history behind us. Have we
seen the important points of this history? Our situation today is
very hard to penetrate, and there is much to endure.

The disclosure of truth and the glorification of the Son is full
of darkness and obscurity. I often feel, sadly, that the official
pronouncements of the various churches are far too harmonious
and insufficiently radical.

Our situation is one of great temptations, confusion and
humiliation. It is a time of great uncertainty. It is gradually becoming clear that the Church has no structures covered by a
guarantee of truth, although we cannot live without structures
and although structures can be (though are not always) good
tools.

Our situation means the opening up of the previous closed
space and the discovery of a new wide-open, dangerous space.
This is a burden we have to bear. In closed space everything was
secure, within reach; there was a familiar metaphysical certainty
which brought with it power, order and subordination. It is no
comfort to be told from various quarters that there can never
"really" be a crisis in the Church; that the only crisis is a "crisis
of obedience". The whole business is much too serious for all of
us to be brushed aside by clerical optimism, from whatever
churches or Christian communities it comes.

The situation is frightening and shocking, and yet the disciples
may be joyful because there is a light which leads to the glorification of Jesus. This glorification means at the same time a rethinking of previous knowledge, which can now be seen as
uncertain. The history of the Church is not a clearly marked
straight path, or organic development; it is a narrow way which
often leads through gorges and battles, confusion and error.
Nevertheless, the promise of the truth has always been there and
is there today. Faith leans on this. And of course faith always involved darkness, was *fides in obscuritate*. Faith and understand-

ing go together; but we can see now that this understanding is often a hard business calling for a rethinking we're not prepared for, and try to evade.

But this time is still a time of promise in which the Spirit is creating new things. In the closed space of our churches, dominated by our inherited attitudes, nothing new could ever happen. In the open, unsafe space God can create new things. That is why this time of the disciples of Jesus is a great time, great even in its all too obvious defeats.

Can we endure this situation? Left on our own, we would have to say that it is far too hard for all of us, far too humiliating, that we are all—or almost all—far too weak, dependent and confused. But in the light of the saying in John we know that something can happen, and something has already begun to happen.

In the truth into which the Spirit is trying to lead us today in a hard school we shall be free, we shall have full authority to search for the truth and find it together: not in denominational isolation, but simply together. In my view, this common search is already a part of the truth into which the Spirit is trying to lead us today.

4. *The problems of today*

Against this background we can look again at the question: Should there be parties in the Church in the future?" But surely the question now has a different ring? Of course there will still be parties. Everything will not be a paradise. Sin will not be rooted out *in via*, and human life, even in the Church, will always be dangerous. The "intelligent spirit of the wilderness" will think up more cunning temptations. And yet our situation has changed. Temptation and promise stand side by side. Has not the time come to look with fresh eyes at our often very lazy denominational "positions", bolted rigid by a tradition which is often questionable? Should we not look at them with a sense of humour? Must we not have the courage to go beyond their venerable but often impossible language? This has nothing to do with false eirenicism, but it has a lot to do with the new situation in which the Spirit of truth is trying to teach us something that will be hard to bear. These are just the conditions for which the promise was given to us, and even if it is not yet possible to move mountains, it is possible to remove some smaller and not so small, even some very large, blocks.

Can we not take the risk of believing (and acting accordingly) that the Spirit of truth is trying to teach us something new today, through our experience in our churches today? The "old days", thank God, will not come back.

We often hear it said that we should start where the differences are not so great, but why not the other way round? Why not start with the white-hot core of the gospel? The question we have to ask is, when Paul in Galatians 1 talks about the one gospel, what can that mean today? Real parties come into being only as a result of complete variance in answering this question. We must begin with the burning questions.

Here I should like to touch on a question that is among the most difficult, the most obviously insuperable problems. When will the parties, which have come closer together at least on the question of the gospel, have the courage to approach the Lord's table together, even if everything is not really clear, even if this were to happen in *obscuritate fidei*? Is the situation not so heavy to bear? Are we not all, from the highest authorities in the Church down to the simplest layman, so exposed, so stripped of our former certainties that we can now go together in the name of Jesus to his table? To put it more modestly, can we not at least consider this and prepare ourselves spiritually for it? Difficult decisions had to be taken in the earliest community, and taken without outside guarantees. In Acts 10 a truly difficult situation is described. Peter took a risk, without security, but in the certainty that it had to be so. After sharing the Lord's table we will have to talk to each other again. Will the conversation then not take another form? Isn't the Lord's table the place where we can learn something new?

The question was, should there be parties in the Church in the future? Ought we instead to speak of different tendencies or wings? I don't think so. There will certainly continue to be parties in the future, that is, disunity in practice, but the parties will be—or have been already—purified of their venom by the blood of the Lord; their power to divide and separate has already been weakened. When we make an effort to understand the gospel, parties are no longer dividing walls but expressions of variety in the understanding of the one gospel.

We are now in a new situation. In its own situation Jerusalem did not take its opportunity (Lk. 19. 41 ff.). Will the same be true of the present situation in our churches and their parties? That must not happen. We must believe and expect that the promise will turn into fulfilment: the Spirit of truth will lead you into all truth, to the glorification of Jesus Christ; even today in our situation which is heavy to bear but full of promise. If our churches are silent, the very stones will cry out (cf. Lk. 19. 40).

Translated by Francis McDonagh

(c) *An Anglican Answer*
Owen Chadwick

I. CHURCH PARTIES IN ENGLAND

"CHURCH PARTIES" was the title of a famous article in the English liberal periodical *Edinburgh Review* for 1853.[1] It caused something of a sensation, for it was the first attempt at a systematic analysis of numbers of high churchmen, low churchmen and broad churchmen in the Church of England. In this article the phrase "broad churchmen", though its use may be first found some six years before,[2] was first popularized and afterwards the phrase was well known to the English public. Together with this went the idea that the Church of England is divided, whether for eternity or not, into three parties: high, low, broad; or those who were church-minded, those who were biblical-minded, and those who were minded towards a restatement of Christian truth in response to the needs of the age; or tradition, Scripture, reason; or Catholic, Protestant, Liberal.

[1] W. J. Conybeare, *Quarterly Review*, 1853, II, p. 330.
[2] Cf. my *Victorian Church*, I, p. 544.

This was a new idea in the Church of England. Of course, the Reformation in England took a conservative course during the sixteenth century with the express object of housing men of different parties in the same Church. Queen Elizabeth I and her advisers wanted a "golden mean" between the extreme to the left and the extreme to the right. In the seventeenth century the historian Thomas Fuller (*Church History of Britain*, IX, section 54) wrote apropos of the English XXXIX Articles of Religion, "Children's clothes ought to be made of the biggest, because afterwards their bodies will grow up to their garments. Thus, the Articles of this Protestant Church, in the infancy thereof, they thought good to draw up in general terms, foreseeing that posterity would grow up to fill the same."

From Fuller's words it is evident that he was already accustomed, if not to parties, at least to wide differences of opinion in one Church. Fuller was upon the edge of the Latitudinarian party; amid so much strife in religion, may we not come to essentials, and allow different modes, even contradictory modes, of interpreting the common creed provided that we do not differ upon the few essentials?

The broad churchmen of the nineteenth century thought of themselves as descended from the Latitude-men of the seventeenth century. But in truth we find a deep difference of attitude. The seventeenth century thought church parties were a lamentable necessity of the vagaries of the human mind. Scaliger said, "All schism is caused by ignorance of grammar." Calixtus said before the Wolfenbüttel consistory, "If all men had the same shape of head, they would all wear the same shape of hat." The nineteenth century had too keen a sense of the nature of human society to believe that parties are caused only by differences of intellectual opinions. They had a more profound sense of historical development. They were aware of the hidden half-conscious elements in the evolution of any society. They were therefore aware, far more aware than their predecessors, of the "non-theological factors" which helped to cause schisms and the diversities of Christian opinion. Scaliger or Fuller supposed that men were different because they thought differently. The nineteenth century was aware that men were different because they had different backgrounds, because their experiences of religion differed, because they made inferences not only from conscious premises but premises of which they were themselves hardly aware.

II. Parties—an Evil or a Way?

The Latitudinarians of the seventeenth century and the broad churchmen of the nineteenth century both realized that the Church, though a divine society, is also a human society and will therefore have a right wing, a left wing and a centre, because such is the law of human societies. The seventeenth century thought that this was a pity and due to human sin. It was an evil, but since it was a necessary evil we must learn to live with it. The nineteenth century was more willing to believe it no sin but an advantage, and a way by which even the Church might make progress.

This sense of "the usefulness of parties" was not confined, during the later part of the nineteenth century, to those who called themselves broad churchmen. From about 1860 onwards we find quite a different attitude to the notion of church parties; not at once frequent or widely diffused, but to be found among thinkers who certainly would have disliked being told that they were broad churchmen, and who often thought the broad churchmen to be superficial. If we ask why this should be so, we find it coming into English thought from two different quarters. On the mainland of Europe these two quarters would have been called the school of Schleiermacher and the school of Hegel. Most Anglican theologians of the nineteenth century were too insular to owe a direct debt either to Schleiermacher or to Hegel. But the movement of men's ideas ran parallel.

(1) The appeal to religious experience carried with it the axiom that words were never fully adequate to describe religious experience. This axiom, baldly stated, was a platitude of all the Christian centuries. The school of religious experience in the third quarter of the nineteenth century inferred that, because no one man could apprehend all the mystery of God, the experience of other men might teach him truths about the mystery which for himself he could not fathom. God is reached, in fact, by partial human apprehension—here in one soul, there in another soul,

each being able to see a shadow of his ways, but often not the same shadow. The Englishman who sold more copies of his theological works than any other English theologian of the century, Westcott, was asked by one of his students whether he did not think that there were two sides to every question. He replied: "Two sides? Surely you cannot conceive of truth as less than a cube?"

We are on the fringe here of the better kind of Liberal Protestantism and its doctrine of revelation as disclosed in an immediacy of personal experience. Such men as Maurice, Westcott and Lightfoot, who dominated Anglican thinking in the later nineteenth century, had a horror of theology that was too tidy, too self-confident, too clear-cut. They were almost distressed by clarity, because they believed that he who was clear could only be clear by misrepresenting God, by bringing the majesty of eternity within the narrow compass of human propositions.

Derived though some of their thought was from some of the broad churchmen who immediately preceded them, their attitude to *party* bore small resemblance to the attitudes of the broad churchmen, still less of the latitude-men of two centuries earlier. It was not at all that men agreed about essentials and argued only about inessentials. Men argued about essentials and were often wrong. But in arguing about essentials they were imagined to provide new insight into truth and thereby to advance the possibility of an apprehension of truth even for their opponents. Men like Maurice or Lightfoot had very little *theoretical* notion of a magisterium in the Church. They sometimes talked as though Christian truth is propagated by the conflicting insights of wise or mystical men. Westcott, for example, expected or hoped that as Hindus were converted to Christianity their specially mystical understanding, derived from their background in Hindu religion, would give Christians a new understanding of St John's Gospel. But although they possessed small theory of an authority speaking in the Church, in practice these dominant Anglican theologians behaved as though they were part of an authoritative tradition. In their biblical commentaries or their dogmatic expositions, even in their historical inquiries, they might use radical methods but they always ended with results manifestly within the lines of Christian orthodoxy. This did more than anything to give them their wide influence among lay people.

(2) The underlying philosophy of these men was not so much Hegelian as Platonic. But their attitudes to church parties were strengthened by the English and Scottish neo-Hegelian thinkers who became dominant at Oxford University during the eighteen-seventies and for forty or more years thereafter were the chief force in British philosophical thinking. Certainly the idea that religious truth was reached by thesis-antithesis-synthesis, was never powerful in British theology. But the existence of this philosophical background probably helped to create the environment whereby men cheerfully accepted such a theological proposition as this: "men are usually right in what they affirm, wrong in what they deny".

Of course these potent but vague ideas did not silence the strife of tongues. Evangelicals and Anglo-Catholics often denounced each other with ferocity, and both evangelicals and Anglo-Catholics were very hot against broad churchmen and as they acquired the title of "Modernists". In Church House, Westminster (the official meeting-hall of the Church of England, hard by Westminster Abbey), on 16 June 1904, a government commission was sitting in a room on the ground floor, with the object of finding some means by which the bishops could repress the wilder excesses of ritualists. Upstairs above their heads the English Church Union, the chief Anglo-Catholic Society, was meeting with the object of encouraging Catholic ritual and denouncing the government's commission and "invertebrate bishops". In a third room the most radical and indeed the maddest of the higher critics of the Old Testament, Professor Cheyne, was lecturing with passion to a conference of broad churchmen. Because the speeches were made simultaneously in different parts of the same official building, it did not follow that the language was more moderate.

III. A Bridge Church

With the rise of the ecumenical movement during this century, a new point or claim was brought into Anglican self-examination. Anglican bishops like Temple or Bell or Headlam were very prominent in the early stages of the ecumenical organizations. The effect of ecumenical meetings on church leaders was to force them to define what was distinctive about their Church and almost to answer the strange question, "What do you think to be your special contribution to Christendom?" Confronted by this question, some Anglican leaders developed the idea of a "bridge church". The Church of England, they claimed, had successfully retained within one organized body both the descendants of Newman and the descendants of Calvin; both those who call themselves Catholic and those who suspect the word Catholic; both those who were proud of the name Protestant and those who detested the name Protestant; both those for whom bishops were a convenience and disliked the words apostolic succession, and those for whom an episcopal succession was of the essence of a valid ministry and a true church. Such ecumenical Anglicans claimed that they showed Catholic and Protestant Christendom how, despite their disunities from Reformation and Counter-Reformation, it was still possible to be one. This was not presented merely as a constitutional achievement, or useful ecclesiastical expedient. It had a touch in it of the nineteenth-century theology—the Church of the future needs Catholic sacramentalism and cannot do without it, it needs Protestant preaching and cannot do without it. In this way the church parties were presented as indispensable to the fullness of Christendom. Thus Bishop Stephen Neill wrote (*Anglicanism*, 1958, p. 387): "In this ecumenical setting, the Anglican churches are sometimes seen to advantage as *par excellence* the ecumenical churches. With their own diversity and variety of traditions, they reach out in all directions, can find themselves at home with all manner of churches, and can to some extent serve as interpreters to one another of widely divided churches both within and outside the ecumenical fellowship."

The argument was never wholly persuasive to those outside the Anglican communion. It altogether failed to persuade some weighty theologians within Anglicanism. Yet there is at least no doubt that the particular history of church parties in England and the various attitudes towards those parties, has lent a special depth and even intensity to the ecumenical endeavours of Anglican leaders, even though these ideas may have spread little among the ordinary men and women in Anglican pews.

Under discussion at the present time is how far the relative tolerance of diverse traditions within one communion is due to a particular and historic relationship with the State. The Anglicans have this special relationship with the State only in England. Elsewhere in the former British Empire they have various traditions within single churches, because all these churches rose from a common English origin. But in the Episcopal Church of the United States, for example, the difference of tradition runs according to the difference of diocese, so that there are "high church dioceses" and "low church dioceses". Where the Anglicans were formerly an established Church, and were then "disestablished"—as in Wales and Ireland—the effect is a certain narrowing of the range of opinion within a self-governing Church. Autonomous organs of church government allow a majority to override, whether in doctrinal definition or in ecclesiastical practice, the wishes of a small minority. In Ireland it became rather more difficult for high churchmen to sit comfortably, in Wales it became a little more difficult for low churchmen to sit comfortably. These observations give rise to argument whether the development of autonomy within the Church of England itself must slowly lead to a certain narrowing of its borders. The legal nexus with the State was intended in the Reformation to protect minorities, though not extreme minorities. As the legal nexus with the State weakens in the modern age, the minorities begin to wonder whether they will be as secure under the self-government of a synodical majority. The Victorian prime minister who was persuaded to do most for the constitutional autonomy of the Church of England, Lord Aberdeen, did so reluctantly. He was sure that the consequence of autonomy must be schism, because the church parties would carry their disagreements into such tension that two (or more) churches would be needed. "The Church of England", said Lord Aberdeen in 1853, "is *two* churches only held together by external forces. This unnatural apparent-union cannot last long, but we may as well defer the separation as long as possible." Though Lord Aberdeen was too pessimistic, it is clear that the Anglican contribution to ideas about church parties owed something to the special historical circumstances in which the relation between Church and State developed from the Reformation onwards.

IV. ADVANTAGES AND RISKS

Ecclesia semper reformanda—Reformers are always needed and always cause trouble. *Ecclesia semper cadem*—someone has to make sure that the reformers in their ardour for change do not throw out the baby with the bath water, and that the changes which they want will end in something better and not in something merely different. *Ecclesia semper pacifica*—someone has to reconcile the points of view and prevent radical and conservative from moving so far apart that they cannot even understand one another. If the Church is ever to be reformed, lest it sink back into complacency and comfort with the world, it is the vocation of the Catholic Church to risk schism from time to time. If it is the vocation of the Catholic Church to risk schism from time to time, it must also be the destiny of the Catholic Church that schism should happen from time to time. The broad Anglican doctrine that Catholic and Protestant parties ought to be able to exist within the same Church did not prevent the Church of England from suffering a series of schisms. It lost recusants to Rome in the sixteenth century, Baptists and Congregationalists and Non-jurors in the seventeenth century and Methodists in the eighteenth century. The Church has to be something. Though it has been compared to Noah's ark, it cannot serve the purpose of Noah's ark, since if all the animals tried to get inside the decks there would be space neither to eat nor rest. A Church which encouraged all possible opinions to be taught would not be the Church of Christ.

Parties must exist. If they did not exist, there would be something wrong about the Church. It would be an artificial society, not a real society of flesh and blood.

Parties bear with them the risk of partisanship, of one-sidedness, of narrow and blinkered views, and finally of schism. In the separatist trends are driven so far that they end in separation, the narrowness and one-sidedness has the less chance of being remedied and can indeed become consecrated. If the parties refuse to divide but remain within the common organization, they fertilize each other, influence each other's narrowness, widen each other's vision and so become fruitful.

In secular states men have sought for a constitution which enables the State to survive without being torn apart by its parties. Occasionally, when on the brink of civil war, they have believed that an absolute government is the only form of government powerful enough to hold the State together between the movements which are pulling apart so far and so fast as to destroy it. But for the most part, in civilized societies, they seek constitutions which will allow parties to manoeuvre and to influence the State in such a way that change is allowed to occur without riot or explosion, majorities rule without trampling on minorities, and conservative men can still feel that the values for which they stand are being in the main preserved.

In so far as it is a human society, the Church needs some such constitution which will allow development without explosion. But the Church seeks such a constitution in certain conditions unlike the conditions in a secular state. It has an apostolic ministry, it has the authority to speak the truth and declare the Scripture, it remembers the song of the *Magnificat* and is not always quite sure whether at times a turning of the world upside down is not after all the best way of change. Within these limits it needs a constitution which can adapt and be adapted. Yet it is at last aware that its constitution, like itself, stands under the judgment of God.

(d) *A Catholic Answer*

Daniel O'Hanlon

FROM all that has been said in the articles which form the body of this number it has surely become evident that the word "party" may be used in many ways. Some kinds of parties are clearly unacceptable in the Christian Church. Other kinds of parties (whether they be given that name or some other less ambiguous one) seem to be just as clearly acceptable, indeed desirable. There are, finally, parties about which it is not so easy to say whether they are a good or a bad thing in the Church. Let us deal with these different alternatives one by one, leaving the most problematical one to the last.

I. Unacceptable and Acceptable Parties

What kinds of parties have no place in the Church? *Any party which breaks communion with the rest of the Church is incompatible with the nature of the Christian Church.* This can happen within one of the churches, as for instance, when one group of Catholics is alienated from another and rejects the other. It can also happen between the several Christian churches, as indeed, for all the ecumenical progress which has been made, is still the case today. Normally the rejection between such parties is mutual. However the process begins, it usually concludes with both parties rejecting each other. Such parties, then, lead to division and a rupture of that communion which is central to the reality of the Church.

It is not difference, but alienation and mutual rejection which turns these two communities into parties of the kind which are incompatible with authentic Christianity. It is the absence of communion which makes and maintains such parties. They should not exist in the Church.

If the only kinds of parties in the Church were the kind just described, it would be easy to say whether or not there should be parties in the Church in the future. The answer would be a clear No.

But it is possible to understand parties in a different and more positive sense which makes them acceptable and even desirable in the Church. If parties are groups in the Church which are *different from each other, not in conflict with each other, and in communion with each other*, they represent a healthy diversity in the life of the Church. Indeed, their absence would be a dangerous sign. What would be some examples of such diversity? One could speak of those who work together for liturgical reform in the Church as a party. The same could be said of the biblical movement, the catechetical movement and the movement for peace and justice. Parties in this sense are really prophetic movements and are a *sine qua non* of renewal and reform in the Church. There is also a sense in which the different religious orders in the Church are parties. National groupings in the Church too, each bringing to the Church the contribution of its own particular genius, can be thought of as parties. Within each nation, particularly those with large immigrant groups, various ethnic and cultural groups can also be parties in the Church in a good sense. In the Church in the United States, for instance, the needs and the special contribution of the black and brown communities can give rise to healthy party groupings.

In the Church of the future it is quite conceivable that the differences between Catholics, Orthodox, Anglicans and Protestants of varying traditions can become parties in this legitimate sense—groups which are different, yet no longer, as at present, alienated from each other, but rather in full communion with each other. If we look even farther into the future, we might even conceive of the possibility of such groups as Hindu Christians and Buddhist Christians, bringing to the Church the wealth of their ancient religious traditions which have found their fulfilment and completion in Christ. But that is a chapter which has hardly begun, and in any case, one which has a completely different prehistory from the one dealing with the different Christian churches and their relations to each other. The mutual excommunications which divided Christians into different churches created alienations which have no parallel in the relation of the Christian Church to the great religions of the East. For a family quarrel has a kind of bitterness and intensity which gives rise to a situation quite different from that of strangers with separate histories whose lives finally begin to intermingle.

These two kinds of parties, then, are not too difficult to evaluate. The first kind, which creates alienation and division in the Christian community, has to be rejected. Such parties should not exist in the Church of the future. The second kind, which brings a variety of groups into fruitful interaction yet maintains communion among them, raises many particular questions about which much more needs to be said, yet in its main lines is not only permissible, but one of the richest potential sources of vitality for the united Church of the future.

II. QUESTIONABLE PARTIES

It is when we come to a third kind of party that it becomes more difficult to say whether or not they should exist in the Church of the future. These are *parties which remain in communion with each other but are in conflict with each other.* At first that may sound like an impossible combination—communion together with conflict. But a realistic look at life in any human community, including the Church, reveals that communion without conflict is really impossible. The only question is how well the tension is handled, so that conflict does not break the communion and communion does not artificially suppress conflict which needs to be dealt with openly and honestly. Accordingly, it goes without saying that legitimate conflict in the Church has to do with matters which do not touch the essentials of Christian faith.

How are such conflicts resolved? At present such conflicts are resolved almost exclusively by the decision of some kind of hierarchical authority. But unless the Second Vatican Council was a gigantic hoax, the Roman Catholic Church has committed itself to extensive participation of the whole church membership in all significant aspects of the Church's life. That calls for the involvement of the laity in a way which has been unknown in the Roman Catholic Church for centuries. How is that to be achieved?

One of the ways might be the introduction of elections and limited terms of office for leaders in the Church, a procedure which could easily lead to the formation of parties in the Church on the model of political parties in the secular civil order. If one looks at the origin of the political parties in the history of modern constitutional democracies, it becomes clear that they are the natural consequence of elections and limited terms of office in combination with the principle of right to free association. In fact, at least one political scientist sees the link between elections and political parties to be so close that the kind of party system —two-party or multi-party—depends on the kind of elections which are held.[1]

To ask the question then, whether there should be the ecclesi-

[1] Maurice Duverger, *Political Parties* (New York, 1963), pp. 216-28, 239-55.

astical equivalent of political parties in the Church is equivalently to raise the question of elections. In other words, parties of this kind and elections are part of the same package. Is it a desirable package? Should there be such parties in the Church of the future? We shall first examine the arguments pro and con and then consider an alternative method of handling conflict in the Church.

III. Arguments in Favour of such Parties

(a) First of all, such parties would involve the laity in the life of the Church on a scale which has perhaps never been achieved before. The plain fact of the matter is that at present, despite statements of principle in Vatican II documents which call for significant involvement of lay people in the life of the Church, the places where such involvement occurs are rare and exceptional. The reason for this lack of lay involvement seems to be that no adequate structures exist to make it possible. Consequently many lay persons, especially the more mature and intelligent, have a sense of powerlessness and frustration. There seems to be no way of making their voices heard, often no way of significantly affecting what happens in their own parish, let alone in their diocese, region, or in the Church as a whole. If there were parties in the Church on the analogy of secular political parties, lay people would have a vehicle for shaping church politics. Indeed, if the Church is to move seriously from the monarchical style which has characterized it for centuries, and is to provide for large-scale participation of all Christians in shaping its life, it is hard to think of a model which seems more likely to bring it about than the model of a church with active parties and elections at regular intervals.

(b) Any argument for parties in the Church must build on the assumption that such parties are not in themselves a bad or an unchristian thing. If one assumes that all politics is a dirty business and that political parties are somehow by their nature contaminated, any suggestion that there be similar parties in the Church will have to be rejected. But is that a legitimate assumption? Can we not argue that political parties are in themselves a good thing, a useful instrument for structuring conflict within a community which has an underlying unity of convictions and ideals? Admittedly, it is possible for political parties to become so ideological that they destroy the basis of community. Such parties would certainly be incompatible with the nature of the Christian Church. But parties need not be of that kind. As long as they remain instruments for ventilating and, through elections, settling conflicts which are perfectly legitimate, conflicts which are in no way incompatible with healthy community, parties might well serve a useful purpose in the Church.

There are those who have no problem in accepting politics as a necessary and good thing in the life of the citizen in secular society. But when it comes to the Church, politics seems out of place, and by some its very existence is denied. During the Second Vatican Council, for instance, one sometimes heard it said that it was not politics which operated in the conciliar process, but the power and guidance of the Holy Spirit. Would it not be more honest to admit that the conciliar process was inevitably political, and that it was precisely through that political process that the power and guidance of the Spirit were operative? And is it not far more likely that these political forces will be more responsible and show greater integrity if they are out in the open? The airing of the issues by clearly identifiable conflicting parties in the Church might make for an open honesty in church politics which has been difficult to achieve without them.

(c) Another value of such parties would be their usefulness as educational instruments: A good campaign in which conflicting parties explain and defend different policies and platforms can be a lively learning experience.

One of the characteristics of the contemporary situation, both outside and inside the Church, is the rapidity with which it changes. The fact of rapid change could argue for parties in the Church, since rapid change calls for frequent adaptation of the Church to changing needs. This adaptation, in turn, requires a serious discussion of the varying and conflicting proposals to implement it. Now if the rank-and-file church membership is to have a voice in evaluating and adopting policies of adaptation to change, organized parties could be effective instruments in bringing this about. At a time when change in the world was very slow, and it was thought right to settle issues in the Church without serious attention to the voice of the laity, no instrument was necessary to involve them in the process. However, with the advent of both rapid change and serious lay responsibility in the Church, new ways need to be found to face this new situation. Organized parties could be one way of getting at the problem.

One final observation should be made before turning to the arguments against organized parties in the Church. The issue here is not a theological but a political one. There are underlying theological issues, it is true, such as that of the basically equal dignity of all Christians and their right to significant participation in the life of the Church. However, such questions as whether this is achieved through organized parties or through processes of consensus without parties are not to be settled through theological argument but by arguments of practical expediency.

IV. ARGUMENTS AGAINST PARTIES

(a) First of all, such parties would tend to institutionalize differences and give them an enduring life beyond the time when they served a useful purpose in the discussion leading up to a group decision.

(b) Furthermore, the open clash of such parties could create lasting personal hostility between individual persons and groups. Admittedly this need not happen. Ideally, Christians should be able to engage in organized conflict over matters of policy without breaking the bond of communion among themselves. But division has been a tragic fact during most of the history of the Church, and we should think twice before encouraging a development which might encourage them and provide them with structural support.

(c) Another consequence of such parties which would be difficult to avoid would be the inhibition or even the breakdown of free communication between them. Given the tendency to polarization which already exists in the contemporary Church, we have a right to be suspicious of any structure which would put people of different minds in separate groups, thus encouraging their tendency to talk only to those with whom they agree.

(d) Probably the consequences of organized parties in the

Church would vary greatly from one region or country to another and be affected strongly by the patterns of secular politics which they experience. Some Christians, for instance, live where there is a long tradition of constitutional democracy with a two-party system. Others live with multi-party systems; still others live in areas of pre-democratic or post-democratic systems or are in the middle of a development towards some form of democracy. In some parts of the world—and not only in Russia and other Communist countries—there is a one-party system. In some countries parties have such a strong ideological character that they conceive of themselves as the only legitimate party and elimination of their rivals seems to be required and co-existence is inconceivable. In other countries where parties have a more pragmatic character, there can be mutual respect for the other's right to exist and the loser is willing to accept the majority decision and support it. To the degree that there is genuine respect of one party for another within the framework of a unified community, a secular political model exists which can be imitated in the Church with some chance of success.

(e) One of the obstacles to the success of a party system in the Church is the inclination of religious people to make everything absolute. Unless it becomes possible, not only in theory but also in fact, to recognize areas of relativity in the Church, every argument about what should be done in the Church becomes one of absolute principle. But once it is recognized that much of church policy and structure is changeable and adaptable, and does not touch the absolute essence of the Church, those who differ about such matters, even if they differ vigorously and argue their difference through organized parties, can still maintain that basic communion which is the Church.

(f) The danger of superficiality is another argument against organized parties in the Church. Once an issue begins to be argued through the mass media the appeal easily verges towards shallowness and sensationalism. But if the Church is a community of the spirit, important decisions need to be made in a quiet spirit of prayerfulness and openness which it is hard to maintain in a popular campaign between competing parties.

V. AN ALTERNATIVE MODEL

Should there be organized parties in the Church to deal with conflict about church politics? There seems to be no compelling argument for or against, and the widely varying implications of such a pattern for different parts of the world complicate the matter even more.

But if it is not through parties that significant large-scale involvement of everyone in the Church is achieved, what can be done to make it possible? *An alternative model could be called the method of consensus or group discernment.* For such a method it is essential that there be a climate of mutual trust and a spirit of prayer and openness to the guidance of the Spirit. Extensive communication is needed, which seems to require that the work be done in groups small enough to make this possible. Ideally, issues would be settled by beginning with small groups at the broadest level and filtering upwards through small groups of representatives at successively higher levels until the level be reached at which the issue is best settled, be it parish, diocesan, regional, national or world level. If this were possible, the community would be working towards a conclusion which was accepted by all, and hence the unity of all would be preserved. Historically, this principle of consensus has been the normal one for settling issues in the Church. Properly used, this method avoids ending up with winners and losers. It has the further advantage of achieving a depth and a responsiveness to the Spirit which easily gets lost in the mass campaigning and debating of organized parties.

Against such a method it can be argued that it seems to gloss over the real fact of conflict and the existence of power groups. It can provide a cover, as does the one-party system in politics, for those who are in control to maintain the *status quo* and effectively block efforts to make another point of view prevail.

This has been an effort to provide *a* Catholic response to the question: "Should there be parties in the Church in the future?" It makes no claim to be *the* Catholic answer. If there is anything which can identify it as characteristically Catholic, it is a concern that the Church be universal enough to have a place for every legitimate kind of variety, yet in such a way that it does not break but rather enriches the communion of all Christians with one another. And in a world which is imploding, thrusting different kinds of people and groups into close contact with each other, perhaps the most precious example the Church can give the world is that of a community of widely different people and groups who love each other, respect each other and manage to live together in peace.

What can we do to overcome Unnecessary Polarizations in the Church?

(a) Léon-Joseph Suenens

THE title of this essay implies the existence of a permissible border-line area open to various inescapable tendencies and emphases. But the essential problem is one of preventing these phenomena from ossifying into a kind of sectarianism instead of sharing in a fruitful interactive process. In short: How can Christians live in sincere intercommunion when they allow themselves to be divided and subdivided for the sake of a whole range of different suasions?

I see only one way of solving the problem: an unceasing concentration on the very foundation of Christian community—our common, living union with one and the same Christ, the Lord and Master of our whole life. For I believe that the answer is to be found in experience itself. Mathematics tells us that two quantities equal to one and the same third quantity are equal to one another. In the Christian perspective, we have to put one basic axiom in first place: Christians will be one, despite all that now divides them, in so far as they respond deeply to the challenge of Christ and his gospel; in so far as they can empty themselves to leave room for Christ as their unity, through them and beyond them as well as in them.

Christianity is not primarily an "ism", an ideology or a system. It is encounter in Jesus Christ with the living God. It postulates the wholehearted living of his basic demand, which is love of God and of one's fellow men; a process which "begins at home". Paul talks of a priority of reciprocal love for the *"domestici fidei"*. That is the primary condition and essential atmosphere for any attempt at union.

Patriarch Athenagoras always insisted, in ecumenical discussions, on that "dialogue of love" which is the wisdom of experience and the "short way" to visible unity. But this actual and reciprocal love must not turn in upon itself; into, as it were, a mere enlargement of the ghetto. As Saint-Exupéry said, "Love doesn't mean looking at one another, but looking together in the same direction".

What we need in order to overcome centrifugal forces is a common perspective on God, and a common perspective on mankind. A truly Christian form of communion and community is like the Saint Gothard tunnel between Switzerland and Italy. To get rid of our conflicts and all the blocks obstructing the tunnel we must have a double intake of fresh air.

In regard to God, the common Father of all the faithful, it is a question of opening ourselves to him, by listening to his word. We have to open ourselves up in common to the message of the gospel; to allow ourselves to be re-evangelized and re-christianized. There is no escaping this demand. We are all, more or less, "sociological" Christians, heirs to the narrow-mindedness of past and present. We have to do a bit of spring-cleaning in order to get down to the evangelical substrate, right under all those encrustations produced by the accidents of history and men's sinfulness. We have to rediscover our primeval and fundamental origins.

This common perspective on God implies listening to God; opening ourselves up to him, and prayer in common. We have to re-learn continually how to say the Our Father honestly, loyally and together. We have to re-learn the breathing into us by the Spirit of that unutterable prayer which he alone inspires. I am sure that the charismatic movement now evident in the Catholic Church and other Christian churches could be of great value in teaching Christians that true prayer which gives unity by virtue of the Spirit. Very often those prayer groups which come out of this spiritual movement bring together Christians of all denominations. For me they are a practical demonstration of an essential unity eluding and cancelling polarizations.

Unity is also necessary in a common perspective on men. We have to respond together to the challenge of the same difficulties and the same hopes of an expectant mankind. This opening up to the world in general relativizes all of us; that is, it gives us a new ratio, a perspective which discloses the main issues of the moment and requires us to concentrate on the essential message of the gospel.

The Church cannot turn in on itself and cannot identify itself with the kingdom of God. But it does have to bring nearer its hour and its advance. Common action among Christians is a sure path towards unity, even though it may not bring about full communion in faith as such. One condition, of course, is that it does not lapse into mere social pragmatism.

This common action is also one of the surest means of discovering one another in truth and of really listening to one another. Such a form of listening is rare because it asks for self-emptying, and wholehearted attention to others; and because it has to be learned gradually.

One has to know how to listen to what is said, but much more often to what is not said: the unvoiced presupposition or subsidiary postulate. Words must be used to get to the deep intention. It is essential to go some way with the others before any discussion. If you want to convince someone else he has to be sure that he is understood, that we have taken in that part of the truth which interests him and which he sets up against us. All men want to be understood in their best parts. As Paul VI said in an address to the Secretariat for Non-Believers: "No dialogue is possible without a deeper understanding of the partner in dialogue, or, as they say nowadays, of the other. This valuable task requires generosity and true asceticism. We have to go beyond the limits imposed by all languages, cultural reflexes and even polemics and distrust in order to open up to abandonment of self and to universality" (*Documentation catholique*, 20, 1972, p. 959). Theologians have already made a serious attempt at reconciliation in the form of the post-conciliar ecumenical dialogue. Fruits of this authentic form of mutual listening are already available— for example, the common documents on baptism and the eucharist. It is desirable that members of the same church should find the right common wavelength so that we can overcome our exclusivisms. It is high time for us to rediscover brotherly unity among Christians; that unity required by the Lord as the very test of our credibility in the world.

Once unity happens at the requisite depth the process of opening up to contrary tendencies will become complementarity. It is not diversity which is wrong, but diversity which ossifies as exclusiveness and refuses to yield to full communion. A diamond is enriched by its many facets. the one light is fragmented. In God, variety is as supreme as unity. Each man's relation to the other is constitutive and congenital and the triumph of his own personality. Reciprocity resides in God, who is undying love. All talk about Christian unity is enlivened by the mystery of the Trinity, which is its source and image.

Translated by John Griffiths

(b) Willem Visser't Hooft

ONE OF the main purposes of the ecumenical movement has always been to transform the tensions and conflicts between the churches into relationships characterized by dialogue, co-operation and mutual enrichment. Now this purpose has been realized to a considerable extent. There is no comparison between the isolation of the churches and their abysmal ignorance about each other which existed fifty years ago and the present situation with its numerous opportunities for contact and fellowship.

But who could have expected that in the meantime the tensions *within* the churches, including those which cut across confessional lines, would grow stronger, so that what we have gained in one area we have lost in another? It seems almost as if a Church Health Organization had successfully dealt with the virus which had caused one form of "rabies theologorum", namely the wild polemic *between* the churches, but had now found that that same virus appeared in a different form, namely that of polarization *within* the churches.

If there is any truth in that diagnosis then the specialists must begin by admitting that they have not done as thorough a job as they thought they had done. They have battled with one form of the illness, not with the illness itself. In other words we have concentrated our attention on what was to happen between the churches in order to arrive at unity, but we did not give sufficient attention to that what was to happen in each church to make it a constructive partner in the building up of the *Una Sancta*. Ecumenism is indivisible. It must begin at home. It is no good loving my far-away brother from another church if I refuse to live in real fellowship with my fellow churchmen. Churches must become uniteable in order to be united. These things have been said before, but they have not entered into the consciousness of the churches. They have often found it easier to engage in inter-church ecumenism rather than to put their own house in order and make peace in their own midst.

But now we cannot escape the conclusion that unless we really develop that "common care for unity" of which Paul speaks (Phil. 2) and develop it at every level we will fail utterly in witnessing to the great *shalom* which is the very *raison d'être* of the Church. It seems to me that there are *three biblical insights* which we need especially to take to heart in order to avoid the kind of polarization which paralyses our churches.

I. A Sense of Proportion

First of all we must rediscover that sense of proportion which characterized the original witnesses. For them unity was unity in the common listening to and following of Jesus Christ. The weight of that common faith is so great that those who hold it belong together even if they disagree concerning some of the consequences to be drawn from the central affirmation. The ecumenical movement owes its very existence to the fact that there is what the Second Vatican Council called a hierarchy of truths. Polarization loses its sharpness and ceases to be dangerous when we remain clearly aware that no discord in the less weighty matters of the faith can divide us as long as we hold on together to the central truth.

At a time of extreme polarization in the Reformed Churches, during the Synod of Dordrecht in the year 1618, the delegation of the Church of England was asked to preach to the synod. The leader of that delegation, the Bishop of Llandaff, felt that this was too risky and refused, but the Dean of Worcester had the courage to accept. He chose as his text: "Be not righteous overmuch, and do not make yourself overwise; why should you destroy yourself?" (Eccles. 7. 16). He said that past centuries had suffered from too much ignorance, but that the present one suffered from knowing too much. The Church Fathers had not been ashamed to confess a certain *docta ignorantia* with regard to difficult theological issues. Paul had said that he did not seek to know anything except Jesus Christ and him crucified. That was the one limit which each theological school should respect. That was a good pastoral care, for it sought to call the polarizers on both sides back to a truer sense of proportion.

II. MANY SPIRITUAL GIFTS

In the second place we must consider more deeply what the diversity of the spiritual gifts means for the life of the Church. Is there any church in the world that has really carried out Paul's programme of the economy of the charismata? And are our polarizations not largely due to the fact that we do not really admit that there are different callings? If in the debate between the verticalists and the horizontalists we would begin by accepting that the Church needs men inspired by the prophetic tradition as well as men chiefly devoted to the cultivation of the spiritual life we would be less inclined to develop one-sided exclusivist theologies. And if we remembered that the church of the New Testament embraces at the same time a Stephen with his radical critique of religious institutions and those who have the charisma of administration (1 Cor. 12. 28) we would not so easily take sides as uncritical defenders or suspicious opponents of the leadership in our churches.

III. MANY EXPRESSIONS OF FAITH

In the third place we must learn to take seriously the plurality of cultures and the corresponding necessity of pluriformity in the expression of the Christian faith. That pluriformity has characterized the Church from the very beginning. The message which Paul and John brought to the Graeco-Roman world was so different in form and language from the gospel preached in Palestine that there was a real danger of polarization. But the polarization was avoided because it was finally recognized that it was basically the same message. We live in a world in which there is such cultural pluralism in the geographical sense, in the sense of diverse generation-cultures, in the sense of sociological groupings, that the gospel is inevitably translated into different cultural idioms. And we find as a result of this growing multiformity tensions developing, particularly between the Western world and the third world and between the generations which can lead to the vicious circle of increasing polarization. How can we resist this polarization? By learning from the original witnesses. I believe that their great achievement is the result of a combination of *three convictions*. Firstly, the gospel was to penetrate into the life of each culture and this required the imaginative and audacious use of the forms of expression characteristic of each culture. Secondly, in doing so the original message must be faithfully transmitted so that it is really the treasure of the gospel which is contained in the new earthen vessels. Thirdly, fellowship in Christ must be maintained between the various Christian families each developing its specific tradition.

IV. Conclusion

There are those who believe that in view of the acute polarization in the churches we must slow down ecumenical development. At first sight, they seem to be right. For how can polarized churches be constructive partners in the ecumenical dialogue? And is there not a real danger that intensive ecumenical contacts will lead to increased polarization in each church? I believe, however, that these questions are now rapidly becoming out of date, for the simple reason that we have reached a point of no return in the ecumenical movement. The time is past when we could make such neat distinctions between internal and external affairs. We are all together in the same ecumenical ship battling with the same tempest. At such a moment we must sink or swim together. We must discover together which are the wrong, the unnecessary polarizations which only succeed in making us introverted and which is the one necessary polarization, not in the

Church, but between the Church and the world. In the early
days of the ecumenical movement there was a slogan: "The
world is too strong for a divided Church". Today we must say:
"The world is too strong for polarized churches". The victory
which according to John overcomes the world is not a polarized
faith but the common faith.

(c) Philip Potter

THE World Council of Churches is "a fellowship of churches
which confess the Lord Jesus Christ as God and Saviour according to the Scriptures and therefore seek to fulfil together their
common calling to the glory of the one God, Father, Son and
Holy Spirit". Over two hundred and sixty churches in some
ninety countries subscribe to this basis and covenant to participate
in this fellowship. They comprise the ancient Eastern Orthodox
churches, as well as the non-Chalcedonian Orthodox churches,
and the Anglican, Protestant and Pentecostalist churches which
have issued from the Reformation of the Western Church. They
span in their origins the Church's history from the first to the
present century. They represent in their life and thought most
of the known cultures and ideological and political systems of
our world. It is in this context that this writer tries to face the
issue posed as to how to overcome unnecessary polarizations in
the Church.

One preliminary comment to be made is that the atmosphere
in which this issue is raised today is quite different from the
atmosphere that prevailed in the period immediately prior to the
Second World War. There are several reasons for this. First, the
age of Christendom is over. The Church is everywhere effectively
a minority in the world and in the nation. Its pretensions of
having a predominant say in society and undisputed sway over
its members are now challenged, though here and there these
pretensions are still asserted. Secondly, the dominance of Europe
and North America is no longer meekly accepted by the rest of

the world. This dominance took the form of imposing theological and ecclesiastical structures of thought and life on other peoples, and therefore of having to claim these structures as eternal dogmas. This dominance has been exposed by the ineffectuality of the churches of Europe and North America to cope with the ideologies and political structures that have been discredited by the events of the past sixty years which have brought us to the brink of nuclear warfare. Moreover, the collusion of the churches with these ideological and political systems has diminished their credibility as the Body of Christ rather than expressions of the body politic. Thirdly, there is now a profound conviction that our church and state divisions and our religious and ideological wars have been brought about by a lack of elasticity of mind and of dialogical existence and by an inability to allow sufficiently for that diversity in thinking, decision-making and acting which is proper to the human species, especially concerning the deepest realities of our being. Fourthly, the growth of the ecumenical movement has demonstrated that the search for the unity of the Church and for the unity of mankind is furthered, not hampered, by a courageous openness of Christians towards each other across our historic confessional and ecclesiastical divisions.

It is the experience of this remarkable development of the ecumenical movement which provides the basis for attempting to answer the question posed about overcoming unnecessary polarizations in the Church. What have we learned from the experience of the World Council of Churches during these twenty-five years? It is important to ask this question because there are many who fear polarization within the fellowship of the Council and see dangers ahead for the ecumenical movement. This concern came to a head during the last Central Committee of the Council when the main theme, "Committed to Fellowship", was discussed. The Letter addressed to the churches, and in particular the four concluding challenges,[1] will provide the framework within which I wish to make the following remarks, bearing in mind the preliminary comment.

[1] *Ecumenical Review*, XXIV, No. 4 (October 1972), pp. 476-8.

I. Open Speaking

We shall have to learn to speak more openly to one another of the centre of our commitment. This centre is certainly "our Lord Jesus Christ as God and Saviour" and is both Christo-centric and Trinitarian. The tragedy of the Church for too long in its turbulent history has been a tendency to prevent or avoid this open speaking with one another. What we have learned from the biblical studies of the last forty years is that even in the New Testament canon there is diversity of expression of the one faith in the one Lord Jesus Christ, a diversity discernible even in one apostle, Paul, as any reader of his epistles would notice. When Paul appeals to the Philippians for unity of mind what he is contesting is not diversity, but selfishness and conceit, on the one hand, and excluding self-interest on the other. He opposes to this the mind of Christ, expressed in his *kenosis*, his self-emptying whereby he became open to men in humble, self-giving love (Phil. 2. 1–11). Polarization is an expression of this conceit and self-regard over against others. This has been the bane of the Church's life and we are only painfully beginning to learn this openness. There is the saying *in dubiis libertas, in necessariis unitas*, but it would be truer to say that the Church has demanded *in necessariis uniformitas* which excludes any real dialogue. *Libertas* and *unitas* are not exclusive of each other.

Our exposure to men of living faiths and ideologies has forced us to realize how much our confessions and theologies are deeply influenced by our cultures and ideologies. It is only through open, fearless dialogue, the "dynamic contact of life with life",[2] that our excluding positions will be unmasked and we shall find new and richer ways of confessing our faith. The New Testament writers were missionary in their intentions and were not speaking within a closed, Christendom position, and so they had the boldness to address the different cultures of their hearers and readers. What is called for is mutual trust among those who hold the same faith in Christ, and a pastoral concern for those who have difficulties to hold this faith but are seeking to keep in dialogue with us.

[2] *International Review of Mission*, Vol. LIX, No. 236 (October 1970), p. 384.

II. HUMBLE LISTENING

We shall have to learn to be better and more humble listeners to one another. This is the direct corollary of speaking openly with each other of the centre of our faith. In his perceptive book, *I and Thou*, Martin Buber writes: "God is the Being that is directly, most nearly, and lastingly, over against us, that may properly only be addressed, not expressed."[3] It is this difference between addressing and expressing which determines our capacity to be humble listeners, for address implies response and therefore responsibility, while expressions (declarations) often prevent dialogue and make for irresponsibility. That is the peril of succumbing to polarization. Man's address to God and God's address to man disclose the deepest levels of their existence. So it must be in man's address to man. And that is precisely what is happening today. Our world is becoming a global parish in which we are all neighbours interrogating each other, seeking to uncover all that divides us as human beings and prevents that community of mind and life for which we all yearn. That is the setting of the threatened polarizations of our time. We cannot shrink from the attitude of address and response, particularly as the fellowship which is given to us is the fellowship of the Holy Spirit whose greatest gift is love.

III. RECONCILIATION

We shall have to learn to comprehend what our Chairman (M. M. Thomas of India) *called "the priestly ministry of liberating reconciliation and the prophetic ministry of liberating conflict".* We will not here enter into a debate about this apparent contradiction. I believe that the reconciliation of which the New Testament speaks is only possible when, through the exposing, liberating gospel, we are enabled freely to face together the conflicts which divide us as churches and as peoples, and submit ourselves humbly to the purifying renewal of the Cross of Christ. This is especially urgent today because the polarizations often mentioned have to do with those issues which divide mankind—economic, political and racial oppression which is often sanctified

[3] Martin Buber, *I and Thou* (Edinburgh), pp. 80-81.

by the structures of society to which churches too often have become captive. It is significant that the Letter to the churches states: "We have not yet found the way to integrate our belief and our action." That is the nerve of the matter. The reconciliation of which the apostle speaks is that by which "we might become the righteousness of God" (2 Cor. 5. 17–21) which embraces the whole life of man.

IV. THE AIM OF ECUMENISM

We shall have to learn to envisage more profoundly, at all levels of church life, the nature and goal of the conciliar process by which the Church has lived down the centuries and into which we seek to enter anew. The most effective means yet devised by which the churches may today avoid unnecessary polarizations is our active commitment to the ecumenical movement, described by the Decree on Ecumenism (*Unitatis Redintegratio*) as "those activities and enterprises which, according to various needs of the Church and opportune occasions, are started and organized for the fostering of unity among Christians".[4] But as the decree itself states at the beginning the aim of the revelation of God in Christ is the redemption of the whole human race. Our experience in the World Council of Churches through these twenty-five years has shown beyond any doubt that through our commitment to fellowship we are driven to face our divisions and polarizations in a spirit of openness and frankness as we seek to be obedient to God's will.

It is a sign of God's grace that in the current polarizations, which cut right across our individual churches, we are still in conversation with each other. There is no going back for us, both as Christians and as churches, from this conciliar process. We can only "pray the Lord of the Church that he will commit us to a dynamic fellowship with him and with all men towards the final fellowship of his Kingdom".[5]

[4] *The Documents of Vatican II*, ed. W. M. Abbott, s.j. (London, 1972), p. 347.
[5] *Ecumenical Review*, XXIV, No. 4 (October 1972), p. 478.

(d) Theodore Hesburgh

POLARIZED Christians, like the poor, we will always have with us. The basic reason is that the Church is a living body, concerned not with abstractions like mathematics, but with living, burning questions like salvation, faith, values and eternity. As Ronald Knox noted in his important book, *Enthusiasm*, the Church has always had those who thought they alone had the pure message of the gospel, they were the *spirituals* or the *gnostici*. All others who did not agree tended to be polarized against them in every age.

Today we seem to use other labels for the same reality—liberals and conservatives in the English language and similar terms in other languages. There is bound to be tension between those who have a different view of growth, progress or even success within the Church and its basic mission. There will always be those who differ about the Church's strategy, organization and priorities in different ages. Some will always insist on tradition while others seek relevance to new problems of a new age. The "signs of the times" may be differently perceived, depending on the point of view of the one who perceives. Even the most basic truths undergo different expression in different ages, languages and cultures.

All this is food for tension, reason for polarization. Against this background, one may more easily postulate what we might do to overcome *unnecessary* tension. I italicize unnecessary because some tension is good and necessary to a vital living body of active concerned Christians. Life would be dull indeed without freedom in the face of possible good and evil, truth and falsehood.

Even granting this, some ages—our own, I believe—are characterized by too much tension and unnecessary polarization. Partly this is true because we are undergoing in a decade changes that normally should have taken place over centuries. Structures are shifting rapidly and those whose lives have depended on the security and changelessness of set structures are shaken, even angry, and polarized against each new change. A new freedom to formulate, to theorize theologically and philosophically and to react to a rapidly changing world have given birth to new centres around which polarization quickly takes place.

My solution is so simple that it may seem simplistic:

1. Let us realize that, more than anyone else, it is the *Holy Spirit* who is at the heart of the Church's life, progress and change. No one has to be responsible for everyone everywhere and all the time—except God, and he, for all of us in these troubled times, is the Holy Spirit, sent by Our Lord to inspire, guide, strengthen and comfort us.

2. *Openness to the Spirit* is the order of the day. Since we are not all that good at always discerning the true Spirit, wherever he breathes—and admittedly he makes it difficult for each of us at times, let us then pray daily to be open to his inspiration and faithful to his guidance as best we can singly and together discern it.

3. Let us be *more understanding of one another when we differ*, together in love, modest about our own special wisdom, quick to admit our fragile fallibility and ready to cherish the true and the good wherever we may find it.

4. Let us practise more often the *Gamaliel principle*, especially when encountering new and unfamiliar ways of Christian attitude or action: "If this enterprise, this movement of theirs, is of human origin it will break up of its own accord; but if it does in fact come from God, you will not only not be able to destroy them, but you might even find yourself fighting against God" (Acts 5. 39).

5. Lastly, let us practise *Christian peace* in our own hearts, confident in Our Lord's love for us and, hopefully, ours for him, and then let us radiate that peace towards all others. Again, he has told us so simply: "Peace I bequeath to you, my own peace I give to you, a peace the world cannot give, this is my gift to you. Do not let your hearts be troubled or afraid" (John 14. 27).

Practice of these five points will not eliminate polarization in the Church, but it may help overcome that polarization which is both unnecessary and unproductive—not to mention, unchristian.

Hans Küng

Parties in the Church?
A Summary of the Discussion

THE question is given different answers for different periods (New Testament, early Church, Middle Ages, Reformation, present) by different academic disciplines (politics and sociology, exegesis and history, systematic and pastoral theology) and by members of different confessions (Orthodox, Lutheran, Reformed, Anglican, Free Church, Catholic). Individual emphases vary widely.

A comprehensive and generally convincing answer seems difficult. On the other hand, the present distress of the churches in general and of the Catholic Church in particular calls for urgent efforts to examine and compare the conclusions of political scientists, exegetes, historians, theologians and practitioners of all tendencies, to see if a consensus already exists or is at least in sight.[1]

I. DEFINING THE PROBLEM

1. Parties in the Church are a real problem

We fully expected some of the contributors to reject the problem of parties in the Church, either because they thought that it did not really exist in some churches now or in the early or medieval Church or because the question was simply unaccept-

[1] My colleagues in the Institute for Ecumenical Research at the University of Tübingen, Dr Hermann Häring and my doctoral student Karl-Josef Kuschel, have read and discussed all the articles in this issue of *Concilium* with me. The subject was also discussed earlier in our doctoral students' colloquium, in which Professor Dr Theodor Eschenburg, among others, took part.

able on theological grounds, parties in the Church being *a priori* a sin against the unity of the Church.

In fact, all the contributors, however they see the solution, agree that parties in the Church are a real problem. Indeed, the specialists in this sphere (Suenens, Visser't Hooft, Potter, Hesburgh) point out or take for granted that we are facing new polarizations in the Church. New tensions in the churches have replaced old tensions between the churches. These new tensions are problematical, but they also reveal new possibilities for ecumenism (Visser't Hooft, Skydsgaard, Nissiotis, Potter, O'Hanlon, Modras, referring to sociological research). Even in the Catholic Church which, in the period from the Counter-Reformation to Vatican II, had a monolithic structure, strong polarizations and parties in one form or another are at least possible. The word "party" is used here in the broad sense of "tendency", "movement", "group" or "wing", whereas in section IV it will be used in the narrower sense of "political" party.

2. *The question is sharpened by the convergence of theological and sociological approaches*

From the point of view of theology, the Church has a special commitment to unity. This is stressed by all the contributors. Because of its basic Christian programme, the Christian community cannot accept barriers of class, race, culture or education, but attempts instead to include tensions and contradictions (Skydsgaard) that are socio-political ("master-slave"), cultural ("Greek-barbarian") and sexual ("man-woman"). This all-embracing unity is already basically achieved and manifested in eucharistic communion (Nissiotis). From the point of view of sociology, however, the Church is also a human organization and not exempt from the sociological laws which bind all human organizations (Eschenburg, Chadwick, Nissiotis, Modras, O'Hanlon), and for this reason the possibility of parties in the Church cannot be excluded in advance.

In its sharpest form, the question runs as follows: Can a community whose aim is to embrace and transcend parties in society, including modern political parties, admit parties within itself, ecclesial parties?

3. Theological, liturgical and disciplinary pluralism in the Church is legitimate

There is also false unity (Skydsgaard). Pluralism can be a source of freedom and creativity in the Church. The diamond of Christian truth has many facets; difference is not bad, only difference hardened into exclusiveness (Suenens). Since the Second Vatican Council, the need and value of a complex pluralism is no longer disputed even within the Catholic Church, but vigorously affirmed: diversity in teaching, liturgy and organization, arising out of diversity in language, culture and ways of thought, philosophical and cultural categories, different religious experiences and different selections from the New Testament (Modras, Hesburgh, Potter). On all sides, and most strongly from the Eastern (Nissiotis, Kéramé) and Anglican churches (Chadwick), there is a desire, not for a uniform, but for a pluriform Church.

In this quarter, then, there are no obstacles to allowing the application to the Church of terms such as "movement", "group", "tendency" and "wing". Parties (in the broad sense) in the Church are acceptable without qualification (and even to some extent desirable) when this term covers groups which differ from each other and are not in conflict, but in communion with each other. These movements may be missionary, biblical, liturgical or catechetical. They may be movements for peace and justice, national, ethnic, racial and social groupings, different religious orders or communities, associations and organizations of all sorts. There will be room in the Church of the future for "parties" which bring a variety of groups into fruitful interaction and yet maintain community among them (O'Hanlon, Nissiotis, Chadwick).

4. Pluralism in the Church has limits

Pluralism can be a danger to the unity and continued existence of the Church. Today Protestants too stress more than they did in the past the need for the unity of the Church in the face of so many attempts to further particular interests in the Church (Skydsgaard, Visser't Hooft). Eastern Christians encourage the formation of groupings in the Church provided that they do not separate from the mother-church and set themselves up as churches (Nissiotis). Even the Anglican Church, which openly accepts parties, has some limits—a church in which all possible views could be taught would not be the Church of Christ (Chadwick). Indifferent pluralism would destroy the character of the Church as the community of believers. Pluralism may be accepted, but promiscuity is rejected. A community that wants to survive needs at least a minimum consensus (Modras, Suenens). Just as democracy cannot be abolished in the name of democracy, neither can the plural Church in the name of ecclesial pluralism.

However much the Church may tolerate various movements, groups, tendencies and wings, there is general agreement that it cannot tolerate sects which cut themselves off from it. Definitely unacceptable (and indeed harmful, even if not always easy to eliminate) are parties in the Church which seal themselves off and separate themselves from the community and its faith and life. These parties include all sects, in other words, whether they are based on theology, race, culture. In the Church of the future there can therefore be no parties which bring alienation and dissension into the church community (O'Hanlon).

5. The final criterion of unity and plurality in the Church is Jesus Christ himself

Because of this ambiguity, because many parties are neither definitely acceptable nor definitely unacceptable, but a question, because parties can exist in the Church which remain in community with each other but are also in conflict, further clarification is necessary (O'Hanlon). Notwithstanding any political commitment on the part of the Church or its members, a political ideology, whether Marxist or capitalist, Communist or Fascist, can never be the decisive criterion for the church community (Nissiotis). The decisive criterion for the church community, for the necessary unity and possible plurality, can for the Church of Jesus Christ be only Jesus Christ himself, as the New Testament testifies. Today this point is stressed equally by Catholics (Suenens, Modras, O'Hanlon), Orthodox (Nissiotis) and Protestants (Visser't Hooft, Skydsgaard, Potter), even if it is expressed in different words. Examples of this are "the person and mission of Jesus", "the gospel of Jesus Christ", "the Lord of the Church", which is the "Body of Christ". If, then, the norm for the Church as the community of those who believe in Christ is Christ himself, clearly all dogmas, rites and organizational forms, and all theo-logies and structures, must be open to reform and correction. *Ecclesia semper reformanda* of course presupposes *Ecclesia semper eadem* (Modras, Chadwick), reform without a change of identity.

II. PRINCIPLES OF A SOLUTION

1. *There are groups in the New Testament which can be called parties.*

The Judaism of Jesus' time was already familiar with religious parties. Best known are the *haireseis* or "parties" of the Saddu-cees, Pharisees and Nazarites, groups which took an individual position on certain important religious questions, without re-nouncing their allegiance to Judaism like the heretical (in the negative sense) "sect" of the Samaritans (Pesch).

Therefore the Church, too, which is based on Jesus Christ, has from the beginning existed in various groups, which in contem-porary terminology may certainly be called "parties" (*haireseis*) because they were based on different "teachings". The primitive Jerusalem community has "Hebrews" and "Hellenists", and later the exclusively Jewish Christian group in Jerusalem took a harder line, and insisted on observance of the Jewish law by all. The Antioch Group regarded the Jewish law as abolished in Christ and practised a mission to the Gentiles which ignored the law. There were also further distinctions between the stricter (James) and more liberal (Peter) Jewish Christians, between communities willing to compromise (James's Antioch formula) and the uncom-promising apostle Paul, in whose communities old and perhaps also new parties emerged (though in Corinth they may have been not so much theological parties as factions which grew up around particular individuals on personal grounds).

2. *These parties are not so much the result of human sin as of the preaching of the gospel in a diverse socio-cultural context*

It was inevitable that the preaching of the gospel to all nations and all men should have different results—particularly as regards the form of the preaching and observance of the Jewish law—in areas of traditional Jewish thought and in the wide area of Hellen-istic Judaism in the diaspora. These groupings led to party spirit, opposition and tension in theory and practice which was probably just as strong as what we know today (Pesch, Modras, Visser't Hooft, Potter).

3. *Nevertheless the individual communities remained linked in a unity which did not allow a division in the Church*

The foundation of this unity was confession of one God and one Lord, Jesus Christ, and thus one faith, one baptism and one Lord's Supper. Even the uncompromising Paul warned against divisions (*schismata*), appealed for a common mind, and was in word and deed in the forefront of the fight for the unity of his communities among themselves and with Jerusalem. "Is Christ divided?", was his battle-cry. Nevertheless, right from the beginning this unity was not a matter of uniformity, but consisted in communication between Christian groups, the transmission of different theological traditions, the adaptation of attitudes and argument about Jesus Christ, the standard of faith, who was not the permanent possession of any one group but was constantly having to be rediscovered in new situations (Pesch, Modras, Potter).

4. *As well as the different parties within the church community, there were groups which not only interpreted the gospel differently but preached a different gospel*

To be distinguished from the parties within the Church are the true sects, *haireseis* in the firmly negative sense, which shut themselves up in their own tradition and language and do not communicate with the church community. Not only Paul, but other writers of the New Testament and several Apostolic Fathers, attack such separatist groups (Pesch).

5. *According to the New Testament, the existence of parties in the Church is permitted, not for the sake of divisions, but for the increase of commitment to the Lord and his Church*

The formation of groups is permitted and desired as an aid to unity and communication, for the building up of the community and for mission, and especially for the service of men. The existence of parties of this type with a special commitment gives groups a more definite character but does not destroy unity. It promotes toleration within the Church but does not make it more difficult to excommunicate those who reject communication in the Church (Pesch).

III. The Lessons of History

1. *Throughout the whole history of the Church there have been tendencies, movements, groups and wings*

These groups have tended towards theology or social affairs, church politics or spirituality. There have also been, from the beginning, groups which, because they have emphasized a particular interest, have separated themselves from or have been forced out of the Church (Vogt).

2. *From the fourth century in particular there were in the early medieval Church true parties with a theological basis*

These were not, as in the past, groups with a particular theology sharply distinguished from the Church as a whole. Now the whole episcopate was divided into changing groups which defended their positions with propaganda literature, by furthering special interests or by mutual accusation and changing coalitions. The struggle centred on the filling of episcopal appointments. Nevertheless a permanent secession by large groups was avoided in the fourth century (Vogt).

3. *A common concern can be seen behind the various contradictory theological formulations*

Of great importance for the preservation of church unity amid all the party struggles was the conciliatory policy of various bishops, and especially Athanasius, who avoided blind partiality and never lost sight of the issue which lay behind and beyond disputed formulas. In this way the various parties were able to recognize the different terminology of other parties as possible and legitimate, and no more was asked than acceptance of the Nicene creed and condemnation of the old heresies. And these parties had positive as well as negative results—they contributed to a more comprehensive understanding of the truth. Not only heretical isolationism, but also ultra-orthodox zeal, has often held up the discovery of truth and inflicted fruitless party battles on the Church (Vogt, Modras).

4. *In the complexity of the historical situation, it is difficult to discern the boundary between the true faith and heresy, between a party within the Church and a sect*

Both in the teaching and practice of the Church actual historical situations include an infinity of tendencies and divergences, affinities and tensions, connections and distinctions. Concealed rigorism and reconciled heresy, influence, aggression and delicate balancing factors make a judgment difficult. The ambiguity of the words *hairesis* reflects the ambiguity of situations (Chenu).

5. *Especially since the High Middle Ages, it has been impossible to ignore the socio-economic influences on many movements, parties and even divisions in the Church*

There can be no neat separation between Church and society, theology and politics. Neither churches nor sects, faith or heresy, can be analysed without taking into account their social roots. There is what might be called a sociological justification for heresy. Economic prosperity, the development of free towns and independent universities, the new ideas of class and increased mobility have influenced ecclesiastical and theological parties just as conversely the religious appeal to the people, the gospel for the poor, the idea of brotherhood, the new ethos of work and apocalyptic expectations have influenced social developments and divisions. Evangelical and political movements have often run side by side and they have always depended and reacted on each other, often with mutual confusion (Chenu).

6. *An authoritarian Church provokes opposition from within*

From the High Middle Ages onwards, a very diverse opposition grew up on the part of individuals and groups. It had a socio-economic as well as a spiritual and theological character, and directed itself against a hierarchy which had identified itself with the feudal system and had thereby become rich and authoritarian (Chenu). How dangerous this often ambivalent appeal to the gospel and new social factors was to become, did not become clear until the Late Middle Ages and the Reformation.

7. *The split between East and West was essentially the result of a rejection of the pluralism traditionally practised in the united Church*

Unity in the Western Church came increasingly to be understood as uniformity. This led not only to an internal hardening but also external isolationism, in the form of a slow drift away from the Eastern churches, which finally became a breach which has still not been mended. The existence of Eastern churches which differ in form amongst themselves and have an equal claim with Rome to direct apostolic origin is a challenge to the Western Church, and in particular to the papacy, to re-think plurality in the teaching, liturgy and constitution of the Church and to make room for it in genuinely collegial structures (Kéramé).

8. *Luther saw himself as a reformer within the Church, but was forced to accept a division in the Church for the sake of the gospel*

There can be historical moments in which criticism must be expressed and protest registered in the sharpest possible way. Luther did not want a breach in the community of the Church, but he did want obedience to the gospel. Since this controversy was clearly about essential elements of the Christian message, the result was not the secession of a fringe group but a split, this time down the middle of the Western Church. Parties within the Church became two different expressions of the Christian Church. To this extent we can talk of a "hierarchy of parties", parties based on superficial matters and those based on essentials (Skydsgaard).

9. *The existence of parties within a single church (as notably in the Anglican) is assessed differently even within this church*

The Anglican Church gradually came to be divided into three parties, high, low and broad church. What was still regarded in the seventeenth century as a necessary evil or even sin has since the nineteenth century been regarded as an advantage and an advance, though there have always been protests from Anglo-Catholics. In our own century the Anglican Church has often been put forward as a model of what ecumenical efforts should aim at, as a "bridge church" between different tendencies. However, this argument has not been generally accepted either inside or outside the Anglican Church (Chadwick).

IV. A SYSTEMATIC SOLUTION TODAY

1. *Current terminology is dominated by the concept of political party (i.e., "party" in the narrower sense)*

"Party" in the narrower sense does not today mean a separatist sect, but neither does it mean merely a tendency, movement or group ("party" in the broad sense). A party in the narrower sense has the following characteristics. It seeks to take over and exercise political power, to achieve specific aims in social welfare and prevent others from being achieved. It puts forward programmes and candidates for elections and has a permanent organization (Eschenburg).

2. *Whether such parties should be formed in the Church is not a dogmatic, but primarily a political question*

The history of political parties and their origin is closely connected with the development of the franchise and its extension to broader sections of the population. Where elections are allowed, the formation of parties is a normal development, and they have always been concerned with putting up candidates for parliamentary assemblies and winning elections. As a rule, every parliament has formal groupings (for the orderly conduct of debates and divisions) and parties (at least for electoral purposes). The setting up of collegial or synodal bodies in the Catholic Church in parishes and dioceses, at national and (on a limited scale) universal level, with at least some elected members therefore makes it possible to form organized groups within these bodies and parties for elections to them (Eschenburg, O'Hanlon).

Acceptance or rejection of parties in the narrower sense does, of course, have theological implications. On the one hand, for example, it makes the priesthood of all believers a reality and, on the other, it preserves church unity. But the question as to whether these theological goals should be attained by means of ecclesiastical parties or without them is a practical question (O'Hanlon, Eschenburg). In answering it, however, the political implications of such parties must be borne in mind. There is, for example, a need for an efficient party organization and at least a rudimentary bureaucracy and party propaganda. Members have to be recruited and party activities have to be financed. Parties may acquire a momentum of their own and this can only to a limited degree be regulated by the parent organization (in this case the Church) (Eschenburg).

3. *There are arguments for parties in the Church*

Organized parties in the Church would make it possible: (a) for the laity to share responsibility without the present feeling of impotence and frustration; (b) to settle, in an orderly and public way, the conflicts which cannot be avoided in any healthy society, on the basis of shared convictions and ideals; (c) to educate church members through the information and discussion which goes with the existence of parties. This is of particular importance in a time of rapid social change in the Church and pressure for it to adapt to new situations (O'Hanlon).

4. *There are arguments against parties in the Church*

Organized parties in the Church would make it possible: (a) for particular religious differences to become institutions, be made absolute and be perpetuated; (b) permanent hostility to arise between persons and groups, a weakening and perhaps leading to the collapse of communications between the parties and giving rise to new divisions in the Church; (c) for Church parties to be confused with political parties and systems, which vary so widely in different countries (O'Hanlon).

5. *In particular situations the formation of parties or at least of groups may be unavoidable*

Since the situations in different countries, with different political systems and levels of development, are extremely varied, it is hardly possible to suggest a general solution (O'Hanlon). In the past, an authoritarian and undemocratic church system has often given rise to a sharp polarization, the formation of parties, and even divisions (Kéramé, Chenu) and this may happen again today. Above all, the connection of ecclesiastical authority with established political power and its refusal to accept political or social commitment may lead to the formation of groups engaged in contestation (Nissiotis). Sometimes, as the result of particular traditions and dispositions of power, a particular group uses spiritual (and also legal and financial) power as a subtle or sometimes even brutal means to maintain a *status quo* advantageous to itself and to prevent serious reforms in Church and society. This one-party church is not the best advertisement for unity and order in the Church.

In this way the formation of a group, or eventually an organized party, within the Church may be unavoidable. For example, when bishops in a synod form a bloc, a counter-bloc is almost always formed, and this will in time have effects on the situation in the Church outside the synod. When a central Roman administration attempts to restore its feudal and absolutist power over the Church's teaching and practice in a democratic age, sharp polarizations, internal disaffection of large sections of the population from Rome and open conflicts are to be expected.

6. *If possible, organized groups and parties in the Church should be avoided*

From a political point of view, it is not certain whether the advantages to Church and mankind of group and party formation outweigh the disadvantages (O'Hanlon). Certainly the tactics, propaganda and the campaigning methods used by political parties can hardly be a model for the Church (Eschenburg).

From the theological point of view, it is appropriate that a community whose aim is to embrace and transcend social antagonisms and political parties should not add its own (inter-church or intra-church) antagonisms to those of society. In some circumstances these take the form of hot or cold wars of religion. It is better for a community of faith, love and prayer to express its spiritual unity as free agreement and mutual openness (Potter).

In view of the well-known inadequacies of the political party system, it may be possible to find other, no less effective, models of decision-making for the Church which are more appropriate to it (O'Hanlon). Questions of faith can hardly be solved by purely majority decisions. In any case decisions in church synods have usually been sought through consensus—not a mathematical but moral unanimity—which means leaving disputed questions open. Even during Vatican II, though votes were necessary, efforts were made to reach this sort of unanimity and in spite of the variety of tendencies no parties or fixed groups in the end emerged. As a means of avoiding the undesirable developments of the party system, there might be practical and legal advantages in having direct voting for specific candidates instead of a proportional system with party lists. In this system the fundamental choice could be limited to the local community or small region, and representatives to the synods chosen from the local and regional assemblies.

7. *Pluralism between churches could become pluralism within the Church*

Even if the formation of groups and parties in the churches is often unavoidable in practice, the terrible experiences of the past make it vital to avoid fundamental divisions in the Church—even for the sake of the gospel. The unfortunate handling by both sides of the Reformation should not be taken by either side as a model for future cases.

The old days must not return. Today all the various churches seek together and concentrate on the essence of the gospel as a means to give scope to the diversity of understanding of the one gospel (Skydsgaard, Potter). Ecumenism is indivisible. It applies *ad intra* and *ad extra*, and must start in its own church if it wants to enlighten the *oikoumenē* (Visser't Hooft). We should work towards a situation in which distinctions between Catholics, Orthodox, Anglicans and Protestants of various tendencies become parties or tendencies within the Church, groups which are different, but no longer far apart, but rather in full community with each other (Modras, O'Hanlon). At this stage a common celebration of the Lord's Supper by the different churches should be considered (Skydsgaard). At the same time, and with an eye to the more distant future and the other great world religions, the possibility should also be considered of recognizing Hindu Christians and Buddhist Christians with their rich traditions (critically examined) within one Christian Church (O'Hanlon).

What has to be done to overcome polarizations in the churches and between the churches? We must expose ourselves fully to Christ and his gospel and together look at God and our fellow men and accept all the consequences of this attitude. We must be open to the Spirit and in sympathy with each other whenever we differ (Hesburgh). We must learn to speak more freely to each other and to listen to each other in vital questions of faith (Potter). We must keep a sense of proportion, which was so characteristic of the first Christian witnesses, have a deeper understanding of the different spiritual gifts with their importance for the life of the Church as against one-sided and exclusive theologies, and take seriously the plurality of cultures and the resulting pluriformity in the expression of the Christian faith (Visser't Hooft). We must try to understand more deeply the conciliar process through which the Church lived in the past and in which it will find new life (Potter). We must practise, together with the priestly ministry of liberating reconciliation, the prophetic ministry of liberating conflict and learn to conquer all conflicts which divide the Church and the nations in the last resort through the Cross of Christ (Potter).

Translated by Francis McDonagh

Biographical Notes

OWEN CHADWICK was born in 1916. He studied at Cambridge University. He has been professor of modern history at Cambridge since 1968 and was president of the Church and State Commission (1966–1970). Among his published works are *The Reformation* ([7]1973) and *The Victorian Church* (two vols., [2]1971).

MARIE-DOMINIQUE CHENU, O.P., was born in 1895 and was rector at Le Saulchoir (Paris), professor at the faculty of Catholic theology at the Sorbonne and a member of the Philosophical Society of Louvain and of the Medieval Academy of America; among his books are *Introduction à l'étude de saint Thomas* (Paris, 1950); *La théologie au XIIe siècle* (Paris, 1957) and a collection of studies, *L'Évangile dans le temps* (Paris, 1964).

THEODOR ESCHENBURG was born in Kiel in 1904. He studied history, administrative law and political economy at Tübingen and Berlin, where he graduated in 1928 in history. From 1929 until 1945 he worked as a scientific expert and executive in industry; in 1946 as a civil servant in the formation of the new Länder; from 1947 as counsellor and representative of the minister for home affairs in Württemberg–Hohenzollern and in 1951 as a privy councillor. From 1946, he lectured in political science at Tübingen, becoming an honorary professor there in 1949, an ordinary professor in 1952 and the rector of the university in 1961, a post which he held until 1963. He is co-editor of the *Vierteljahreshefte für Zeitgeschichte* and a regular contributor to the weekly newspaper *Die Zeit*. His published works include: *Das Kaiserreich am Scheideweg—Bassermann, Bülow und der Block* (Berlin, 1929); *Der Beamte in Partei und Parlament* (Frankfurt a.M., 1952); *Herrschaft der Verbände?* (Stuttgart, 1955); *Die deutschen Fragen* (Munich, 1959); *Der Sold des Politikers* (Stuttgart, 1959); *Das isolierte Berlin* (Tübingen, 1960); *Ämterpatronage* (Stuttgart, 1961); *Probleme der modernen Parteifinanzierung* (Tübingen, 1961); *Staat und Gesellschaft in Deutschland* (Piper, Munich, 2nd edn., 1963); *Zur politischen Praxis in der Bundesrepublik* (Munich, I, 1964; II, 1966; III, 1972); *Die improvisierte Demokratie* (Munich, 1963); *Über Autorität* (Frankfurt a.M., 1965); *Matthias Erzberger* (Munich, 1973).

THEODORE M. HESBURGH, c.s.c., born in 1917, ordained in 1943, studied at Notre Dame and received degrees from the Gregorian University in Rome, Holy Cross College and the Catholic University of America in Washington D.C. He has been president of the University of Notre Dame since 1952 and has served on many national and international boards and committees. At present, he is Chairman of the Academic Council for the Ecumenical Institute for Advanced Theological Studies in Jerusalem; Chairman of the Overseas Development Council; a member of the Carnegie Commission on Higher Education, the Board of Trustees of the Rockefeller Foundation and several other foundations and institutes. He has served as a member of the U.S. Commission on Civil Rights from 1957 to 1972 and was Chairman of the Commission from 1969 to 1972. He is the author of several books on theology and on education, among them, *God and the World of Man* (1950); *Patterns for Educational Growth* (1958); *Thoughts for Our Times* (³1969).

WILLEM VISSER'T HOOFT, born in 1900 at Haarlem (The Netherlands), Protestant, studied at the University of Leiden, gaining his theological doctorate (1928). He was Secretary to the World Alliance of Y.M.C.A.s, Geneva (1924–1938) and General Secretary to the World Council of Churches, Geneva (1938–1966). He is honorary D.D. of several American, Asian and European universities. His publications include: *No Other Gods* (1937); *The Church and Its Functions in Society* (1937), with J. H. Oldham; *The Struggle of the Dutch Church* (1946); *The Meaning of Ecumenical* (1953); *The Renewal of the Church* (1957); *Rembrandt and the Gospel* (1957); *No Other Name* (1963); *Peace amongst Christians* (1967)—with Cardinal Bea.

ORESTE KÉRAMÉ, born at Beirut in 1895, is a Melkite Catholic, ordained in 1924. He studied at the Jesuit scholasticates in Jersey and Hastings. He was adviser to Patriarch Maximos IV at Vatican II and has taught Eastern theology at New York, Washington and Boston. At present, he is Archbishop Joseph Torvil's personal adviser and exarch for the Melkites in the United States. Among his published works are: *Notre vocation et notre âme de chrétien d'Orient* (Le Lien, 1954); *Constantinople et le Grand Schisme Chrétien* (Le Lien, 1954); *Le Prochain Concile. Catholiques et Orthodoxes bientôt réunis?* (Beirut, 1960).

HANS KÜNG, born in 1928 in Sursee (Switzerland), is professor of dogmatic and ecumenical theology and director of the Institute for Ecumenical Research at the University of Tübingen. Among his works are: *The Church* (1968); *Infallible? An Enquiry* (1971); *Menschwerdung Gottes* (1970); *Why Priests?* (1972); *Fehlbar?* (1973).

RONALD MODRAS was born in 1937 in Detroit, Michigan (U.S.A.) and ordained in 1963. He studied at Tübingen, where he obtained his doctorate in systematic theology. He is a professor at St John's Seminary (Plymouth, Michigan) and an adjunct professor at the University of Detroit. His published works include a variety of articles and *Paths to Unity* (1968).

NIKOS NISSIOTIS was born in Athens in 1925 and is a member of the Greek Orthodox Church. He studied at the Universities of Athens, Zürich, Basle and Louvain, gaining his diploma in philosophy and his doctorate in theology (1956). Since 1965, he has been teaching as a professor of the philosophy of religion at the theological faculty of the University of Athens. He has been director of the de Bossey Ecumenical Institute (Switzerland) since 1966. His publications include *Philosophie de la religion et théologie philosophique* (1965). He is the author of various articles on ecumenical dialogue, ecumenism and the Orthodox Church and on the Vatican II Decree on Ecumenism.

DANIEL O'HANLON was born in 1919, joined the Jesuits in 1939 and was ordained in 1952. He studied at Loyola University, Los Angeles, in the Philosophical Faculty of Gonzaga University, Spokane, the Gregorian University and the Universities of Dublin, Fribourg and Tübingen, gaining his M.A. in philosophy and his doctorate in theology. A specialist in ecumenical questions, he co-edited with Yves Congar and Hans Küng *The Council Speeches of Vatican II* (London and Melbourne, 1964) and he is also co-editor of *Christianity Divided* (London and Melbourne, 1962). He is a contributor to *Theological Studies, Cross Currents, Worship, Commonweal* and *America*.

RUDOLF PESCH was born at Bonn in 1936. He studied Catholic theology, history and German at the Universities of Bonn and Freiburg i.Br.; doctor of philosophy (modern history, 1964), doctor of theology (New Testament, 1967); full lecturer in the department of New Testament studies at Innsbruck (1969); from 1971 onwards, he has been professor of Catholic Theology with special reference to biblical studies in the department of religious studies at Frankfurt. His most recent publications include: *Jesu ureigene Taten? Ein Beitrag zur Wunderfrage* (Freiburg, 1970); *Freie Treue. Die Christen und die Ehescheidung* (Freiburg, 1971); *Der Besessene von Gerasa. Entstehung und Überlieferung einer Wundergeschichte* (Stuttgart, 1972); *Die kleine Herde. Zur Theologie der Gemeinde* (Graz, 1973).

PHILIP POTTER, born in Roseau, Dominica, West Indies, in 1921, worked with the Attorney-General of Dominica, and studied law 1938-1943. Served as pre-seminary pastor 1943-1944. Theological studies at Caenwood Theological College, Jamaica, and at Richmond College, London (B.D., 1944-1948). Overseas secretary (including concern for mission) of the British Student Christian Movement (1948-1950). Pastor in charge of Cap Haitien Circuit, Methodist Church, Republic of Haiti (1950-1954). Master of Theology, London University (1954). Secretary and later Executive Secretary, Youth Department, World Council of Churches (1954-1960). Secretary for West Africa and West Indies, Methodist Missionary Society, London (1961-1966). Associate General Secretary, World Council of Churches and Director of Division of World Mission and Evangelism (1966). Chairman, World Student Christian Federation (1960-1968).

KRISTEN EJNER SKYDSGAARD was born in 1902 and ordained in 1935. He gained his doctorate in theology in 1937 (metaphysics and faith) and was a pastor from 1935 until 1970. He was professor in dogmatic and symbolic theology at the University of Copenhagen between 1940 and 1972 and leader of the ecumenical institute there between 1956 and 1972. He was an observer at Vatican II (1963-1965).

LÉON-JOSEPH SUENENS, Primate of Belgium, was born in 1904 at Brussels, ordained in 1927, consecrated bishop in 1945, appointed archbishop of Malines and Brussels in 1961 and made a cardinal in 1962. He studied at the Gregorian in Rome where he obtained his doctorates in philosophy and theology, and a *baccalauréat* in canon law. Among his books are: *L'Église en état de mission* (1955); *Promotion apostolique de la religieuse* (1962); *Coresponsibility in the Church* (1968); *The Future of the Christian Church* (1971) in collaboration with H. Ramsey.

HERMANN-JOSEF VOGT was born near Saarbrücken in 1932. He studied philosophy and theology in Trier and at the Gregorian, and graduated and became a recognized teacher at Bonn; his doctoral thesis was on *Coetus Sanctorum. Der Kirchbegriff des Novatian und die Geschichte seiner Sonderkirche* (Bonn, 1968). He is now professor of patrology and the history of the early Church in the department of Catholic theology at Tübingen.